"I've been waiting a long time to read a book as soulful and precise, in its treatment of listening, as Zachary Pace's tender account of an identity put back together through the powerful elixir of singing women. Pace, a lover of the overlooked, attends to the brocaded minutiae of triumphs, comebacks, travails. To enunciation and excess, Pace brings a curatively lucid eye and ear, each vignette invested with lyric care, and with a fastidious affection for the contours of a singer's career. This impeccable book sends me back, with a renewed heart, to the songs Pace masterfully covers, with a delivery as splendid, as emotionally impressive, as the lauded originals." —**WAYNE KOESTENBAUM**

"What draws us to the sound of another person's voice? What magnetizes others to our own? *I Sing to Use the Waiting* is not only a thrilling homage to a group of majestic women, but an exploration into the nature of voice itself—that queer and primal animal signature. Zachary Pace writes with electric intensity. A total joy." —**PAUL LISICKY**

"Zachary Pace's *I Sing to Use the Waiting* is an exhilarating mix, part memoir, part examination of queer identity, part investigation into corporate heteronormativity and the internalized homophobia it produces in children and others who are still growing into who they are—and so much more, all of it approached via the lenses of the singers (and their lives) whom Pace encountered at pivotal moments in their own growing up. In considering a recording made by Nina Simone, for example, Pace comes to understand voice itself as a form of queerness, straddling registers, enacting a fluidity that refuses binary thinking; other singers—Fiona Apple, Mariah Carey, Joanna Newsom—become a source of actual vocabulary 'for interpreting the world'; and in a discussion of Kim Gordon and Sonic Youth, Pace considers lyrics and music as entryways to the sublime, as a way 'to remember the demise that is my only destiny, relieved I've eluded it for now.' At one point, Pace says of Rihanna's career that it 'enacts a singularly liberating experience of identity expression.' I'd say the same for *I Sing to Use the Waiting*, a beautifully provocative, smart, and tender book indeed." —**CARL PHILLIPS**

I SING TO USE THE WAITING

A Collection of Essays About the <u>Women Singers</u> Who've Made Me Who I Am

ZACHARY PACE

Two Dollar Radio
Books too loud to Ignore

Two Dollar Radio
Books too loud to Ignore

WHO WE ARE TWO DOLLAR RADIO is a family-run outfit dedicated to reaffirming the cultural and artistic spirit of the publishing industry. We aim to do this by presenting bold works of literary merit, each book, individually and collectively, providing a sonic progression that we believe to be too loud to ignore.

TwoDollarRadio.com

Proudly based in
𝕮𝖔𝖑𝖚𝖒𝖇𝖚𝖘
OHIO

 @TwoDollarRadio

@TwoDollarRadio

/TwoDollarRadio

Love the
PLANET?
So do we.

Printed on Rolland Enviro®.
This paper contains 100% sustainable recycled fiber, is manufactured using renewable energy - Biogas and processed chlorine free.

100%   PCF   BIO GAS® ENERGY   PERMANENT

Printed in Canada

SOME RECOMMENDED LOCATIONS FOR READING:
Crying on public transportation, waiting for the show to start, hoping for a crush to call, or pretty much anywhere because books are portable and the perfect technology!

AUTHOR PHOTO→
Jared Buckhiester

COVER PHOTO→ Photo by
Daniel Schludi on Unsplash.
COVER DESIGN→ Eric Obenauf

Two Dollar Radio would like to acknowledge that the land where we live and work is the contemporary territory of multiple Indigenous Nations.

Versions of these essays appeared in the following publications:

"Daddy Was a Musician" in *The Yale Review* (as "My Queer Voice"); "My Tattoos" in *The New Engagement*; "Massage the History" (as "Seeking the Sublime in Sonic Youth") in *Literary Hub*; "Could We" in *The Fanzine*; "I Sing to Use the Waiting" (as "Playback Mode") in *The Baffler*; "Black Is the Colour of My True Love's Hair" in *Wendy's Subway*; "Is Language a Virus?" in *Exquisite Pandemic*.

For Rebecca Sue

I sing to use the Waiting
My Bonnet but to tie
And shut the Door unto my House
No More to do have I

Till His best step approaching
We journey to the Day
And tell each other how We sung
To Keep the Dark away.

—Emily Dickinson

AUTHOR'S NOTE

In quoted material, whenever possible and appropriate, the masculine pronoun has been recast in brackets with gender-neutral pronouns.

CONTENTS

I SING TO USE
THE WAITING

DADDY WAS A MUSICIAN

On My Queer Voice

1.

You can hear, as soon as I start to speak—effeminate inflection, nasal vowels, slight lisp—qualities of tone that may sound dissonant from my gender presentation: a queer voice.

My mother loves to reminisce that even before I learned to walk, every time a certain 1987 Pepsi commercial aired—in which a vending machine opens a portal into a crowded nightclub where Gloria Estefan dances onstage, lip-synching a verse from "Conga" (its lyrics replaced by Pepsi marketing slogans), backed by the members of Miami Sound Machine miming its unmistakable instrumentals—I'd crawl to the television, pull myself up, press my hands against the screen, and bounce exuberantly to the beat of the song.

There, the cultivation of my personality ignited from the incandescence of a woman singing.

Here, let's define *queer*: "*whatever* is at odds with the normal, the legitimate, the dominant"—according to queer theorist David M. Halperin. If we're talking about queer people, then we're primarily referring to people who prefer nonconforming sex and gender presentations.

Now, let's acknowledge that those dominant, legitimized norms have assigned explicit but arbitrary attributes to "masculine" and "feminine" behavior, which queer people transgress.

2.

My father wasn't much of a musician. He was a drummer in high school, but beyond that, he didn't pursue expertise in any instrument, and his singing voice sounded treacly. However, he possessed perfect pitch; he could play, by ear, any given melody on a keyboard, and he claimed to have superior hearing on his left side—his hearing on the right side, damaged during his decades moonlighting as an audio engineer.

To remind us of which side was inflicted with hearing loss, so we'd speak nearer to his better ear, he wore an earring in his right lobe—coincidentally, a signal associated with male homosexuality in the late eighties and early nineties, which provoked my peers to broadcast the rumor that he was queer.

Although he constantly changed employers and professions—from optician to telemarketer—he kept a steady weekend gig as audio engineer for a local country band, and he picked up numerous odd stage-production jobs, most notably for the Rolling Stones's "Steel Wheels" tour in 1990. Once, he boasted that my mother discovered she was pregnant with me while he was working at the inaugural Farm Aid benefit concert of September 1985. But the dates don't corroborate this statement; my somewhat premature birth occurred a full twelve months later.

Such a fixation on music marked my childhood. In a handful of old photographs, he's dressed in one of his Grateful Dead T-shirts and wearing a pair of headphones—sulking, slouched in an armchair next to his turntable and rack of records. I can conjure him vividly in this pensive pose, somberly concentrating, so absorbed he'd virtually dissolve within his listening.

Reared in front of the television, I might have spent as many hours watching Disney musicals as I spent interacting with my parents. Revisiting formative footage from my youth, I recognize many of my mannerisms that originated on TV.

"Your ideas about who you are don't just come from inside you, they come from the culture," says film professor Richard Dyer in *The Celluloid Closet*, a 1995 documentary examining the history of queer characters in American cinema. "In *this* culture, they come especially from the movies, so we learn from the movies what it means to be a man or a woman—what it means to have sexuality."

As the only child of a depressive father and an overworked mother (whose demanding career kept her frequently preoccupied)—in a house without neighbors, in the woods on top of a hill—I was taught by that television, my constant companion, how to be human.

Vito Russo, author of *The Celluloid Closet* (the 1981 book on which the documentary was later based), writes: "The idea of homosexuality first emerged onscreen... as an unseen danger, a reflection of our fears about the perils of tampering with male and female roles... Crucially at issue always was the connection between feminine behavior and inferiority."

Are you a boy or a girl? At age twelve, I was taunted by bullies every day in school—my hair dyed blond and growing past my ears, my mincing gait, my lilting voice. *Are you a boy or a girl?* Every day, I dreaded their mockery.

To this day, talking among strangers—who often look up, with an inquisitive smirk, when I start to speak—I blush, instinctively ashamed of this queer timbre.

3.

What makes a voice sound masculine or feminine, anyway?

Air steadily streams through your open vocal folds (commonly called vocal cords) as you breathe. When your cerebral cortex transmits the idea to phonate, your glottis (the vocal folds' opening) shuts. This airstream stoppage produces an acoustic vibration, which travels through your larynx, pharynx, oral cavity, and nasal cavity, and which your palate, tongue, teeth, and lips then modulate.

The number of times the glottis opens and closes each second, called "phonatory cycles," contributes to the level of the pitch we hear. Measured in hertz, pitch rises as the result of shorter and more frequent phonatory cycles. Conventionally masculine pitch averages 120 hertz, and conventionally feminine pitch averages 225 hertz; male-bodied voices tend to drop an octave during puberty, while female-bodied voices tend to drop a third or half an octave. This happens because the vocal folds of the male body usually grow about a half centimeter longer and thicker than those of the female body, and the male-bodied larynx also tends to grow about a half centimeter larger, forming the Adam's apple.

Out of these minuscule bodily variations, we have created a polarizing binary, binding disparate characteristics to discrete genders.

What makes male-bodied voices sound stereotypically queer? David Thorpe's documentary *Do I Sound Gay?* poses this question. Ron Smyth, a linguistics professor at the University of Toronto, tells Thorpe that "microvariations" typify feminine and masculine pronunciations; for example, effeminate speakers "tend to make their *S* with the tongue in a slightly forward position… Acoustically, that means [that] it sounds higher." Smyth narrows down the queer voice to these components: clearer and longer vowels, a clearer *L* and a longer *S*, and an overarticulated *K*, *P*, and *T*. Thorpe fails to challenge the supremacy of the gender binary—accepting instead the polarization of pitch levels as an irrefutable facet of gender presentation—and the film fails to deliver a groundbreaking explanation for (or defense of) the sonic idiosyncrasies associated with a male body producing a high pitch (quite the contrary: Thorpe seeks lessons from a vocal coach to lower his pitch). Still, the influence of culture on the cultivation of personality resonates. Benjamin Munson, from the department of speech-language-hearing sciences at the University of Minnesota, tells Thorpe that, when learning language, "a kid is identifying: 'Here is a particular speaker, and here is a particular facet of that person's speech that sort of captures what I find so engaging about them, and I'm going to emulate that.'"

And so, while my distant, dismissive father dissociated beside his turntable with his headphones—and while my charismatic, compassionate, savvy, and sophisticated mother worked late, made dinner, cleaned the house, walked the dog, mowed the lawn, paid the bills—I sat before the television, emulating the women performers whom I encountered there: where I'd once commenced that very exuberance, which my mother still loves to recall.

4.

"The break between registers… is the place within one voice where the split between male and female occurs," Wayne Koestenbaum declares in *The Queen's Throat*, a book on the queer proclivity for opera divas. "By revealing the register break, a singer exposes the fault lines inside a body that *pretends* to be only masculine or only feminine" (italics mine).

From the beginning, I sought to emulate these performances of femininity: not only Gloria Estefan's Pepsi commercials but also her *Sesame Street* appearances; Disney princesses, especially Ariel (once, when ill, I lost my voice and was convinced Ursula had stolen it); Mary Martin's role as Peter Pan, my introduction to gender-bending; Judy Garland's Dorothy, my initiation *into* gender-bending (in preschool, playing dress-up, I'd wear a skirt and skip around, chanting "Follow the Yellow Brick Road"); Paula Abdul's single "Will You Marry Me," my first cassette tape; Cher's *Heart of Stone*, my first CD (a gift from my mother's queer friend); Tina Turner's *Tina Live – Private Dancer Tour*, the first televised concert that I watched. I began writing poems at the age of eight because Janet Jackson's recitation of Maya Angelou's poetry in the 1993 film *Poetic Justice* made me want to make words into music, too.

My friends and I fostered our musical tastes with our parents' collections, cable or satellite television, and movies. We waited by the radio or TV to record a song or music video on a blank tape. Using pen and notepad, I'd obsessively transcribe the lyrics to my favorite tunes, editing the misheard lines whenever those songs would grace the airwaves. While I was in college, MP3 players replaced CDs and Discmans, which had replaced cassettes and Walkmans when I was in middle school, and then my friends and I would wait by the computer to download from file-sharing services such as Napster and LimeWire through our dial-up modems and DSL connections.

As I watch that 1987 Pepsi commercial on YouTube now, through Wi-Fi on my smartphone, Gloria Estefan's familiar and inimitable pitch sends me into nostalgia for a mother figure's charismatic compassion, which I associate with my own mother's love of my earliest exuberance.

5.

"My Daddy Was a Musician" is the title given to the bootlegged recordings of an unreleased song by Chan Marshall, who performs and records as Cat Power—and whose enchanting voice, for me, epitomizes this charisma of maternal compassion.

I've tracked down a few renditions of the song, which she played on guitar at solo performances around 2001. It consists of only one chord, A minor, which she strums over and over. This is her habitual technique when playing solo on guitar and piano: She'll hit a root note and then its chord, repeatedly, alternating like footsteps at an adamant pace.

The stanza that gives the song its name both bemoans and embraces the inevitability of inherited traits, genetic fates, and transgenerational traumas:

> *My daddy was a musician*
> *And my granddaddy, too*
> *You know, my mama was a musician*
> *Looks like I'll be a musician, too.*

On the recording from Studio Brussel's *duyster* session of January 2003, Chan's voice exemplifies the quality of tone I love to love again and again—her modulation evenhandedly conveying the simultaneous pain and joy of being human.

The song probably won't be a contender for future studio albums; she repurposed one of its phrases in "Ruin" on her 2012 record, *Sun*, and back in 2005, she replaced "My Daddy" in concerts with a cover of "House of the Rising Sun" (also in A minor), which she recorded in studio for the *Live Session (iTunes Exclusive)* EP released in 2006. Here, she changes a line from the Animals's interpretation of "Rising Sun":

> *My father was a gamblin' man*
> *Down in New Orleans—*

to:

> *My father was a music man*
> *Do you really know what that really means?*

6.

Musically speaking, my father was an amateur.

"[The] Amateur renews his pleasure (*amator:* one who loves and loves again)," writes Roland Barthes, "he is anything but a hero (of creation, of performance)... his praxis, usually, involves no *rubato*..."

I'm particularly partial to the *Oxford English Dictionary*'s definition of *rubato*: "A temporary disregard for strict tempo to allow an expressive quickening or slowing, typically without altering the overall pace."

Rubato resembles queerness: At odds with the tempo's dominance, a performer deviates from a score's presiding rhythm. This practice enables the performer to personalize the phrasing—to create their genius—through improvisation, through playing with pacing. An amateur ardently obeys, observes, internalizes the score, without the genius to recreate it.

Akin to Barthes's amateur, my father maintained an untutored appreciation for music that allowed him to replicate, via listening, whatever original elation he'd derived from it—demonstrated by my foundational elation at the cadence of "Conga"—thus replacing boredom or despair with contentment and continuity.

"Listening, we are the ideal mother... attending to the baby's cries, alert to its puling inscriptions," Koestenbaum concludes in *The Queen's Throat*, "and we are the baby listening to the mother for signs of affection and attention, for reciprocity, for world."

My father and I, being listeners, became escapists, to evade the void of our world, to distract us from its disasters and mundanities. (One night, as my mother crooned to a live performance on a televised awards show, my father hushed her and turned up the volume—disrupting her exuberance, her outward enjoyment, in favor of his private, inward enjoyment.) I've inherited his depression and his trauma, as well as his coping mechanisms and survival tactics.

Listening, I can emote vicariously through the singer, who vocalizes with a confidence I covet—the singer's voice as embodied as mine would be, if mine didn't humiliate me—and often, I do sing along (alone) in cathartic mimicry.

"The gestures of a singer... are delectable because they are so easily imitated," Koestenbaum confides.

In a photograph my father mailed to me while we were still speaking, I'm probably five, clutching a toy microphone with both hands—mid-song, mouth agape—my amorous pose suspended in that ecstatic moment: an articulation of uninhibited pleasure.

In another photograph, I'm a little younger, clutching the same toy microphone, wearing my mother's black leather gloves, with my security blanket draped on my head in imitation of long hair. I don't remember intending to reproduce femininity; it simply was (and is) the natural mode of my gender presentation—except when compelled to masculinize my body language and vocal quality to avoid ridicule.

"[My] body produces homosexuality—sings it, expresses it. I don't have any choice. Homosexuality is the specific music my body makes," Koestenbaum confesses.

But where homosexuality (by default, heterosexuality's supposed inverse) may inadvertently replicate dominant power structures and gender stereotypes, queerness intentionally rephrases and delegitimizes those structures and stereotypes, deviating from the presiding rhythms of sexual and social norms: countercultural rubato.

My foremost comprehension of attraction to the male body took place in preschool. For many years, I didn't have a concept of "gay" or "homosexual"—or "queer," which I'd eventually learn as a curse word—nevertheless, I'd perceived that this attraction was overwhelmingly considered marginal, even abnormal. At one point, I thought my only option for romancing another male would be to cross-dress, because I saw Martin Lawrence do so, in jest, on his TV series, *Martin*.

At age fourteen, I "came out" as bisexual; back then, the designation offered a buffer, permitting me to backpedal into the metaphorical closet in case the backlash proved too unbearable. Tentatively, I identified as gay or homosexual. Now, I unreservedly deem myself queer—and newly prefer to use nonbinary pronouns.

Initially, my father was indignant; he vacillated between insisting *this is a phase* and *this is your mother's fault*.

One night, in the heat of a disagreement, he called me a freak.

That night, feeling exceptionally abandoned and unprotected, I sensed his cruelty would keep reverberating in my self-consciousness. From then on, I would bemoan being perceived as a freak—and have only recently embraced the idea of being a freak.

Eventually, my father conceded that he'd accept my queerness if I produced biological offspring bearing his surname. Decades later, I'm still baffled by the audacity of this ultimatum—designed to legitimize my existence, presented by one of the two people responsible for my existence in the first place.

As our distance increased and contact diminished, we gradually arrived at our present impasse: estrangement.

7.

    My daddy was a musician
    And my granddaddy, too—

I believe these lines are literal for Chan Marshall. Raised in a family of aspiring musicians, she followed their lead and then found her own path as a world-renowned professional singer, instrumentalist, and songwriter.

But when I say that my daddy was a musician, I mean my father's homophobia spawned my most self-hating, self-punishing instincts, and I believe his homophobia was the spawn of his own self-hating, self-punishing instincts, which were spawned by the homophobia of his father (whom I have reason to suspect was secretly queer)—the trauma of generation upon generation of rejecting queerness.

David Halperin's *Saint Foucault*—the source of my introductory definition of *queer*—suggests that queerness can provide "a positionality that is not restricted to lesbians and gay men but is in fact available to anyone who is or who feels marginalized because of her or his sexual practices." Halperin encourages us to "envision a variety of possibilities for reordering the relations among sexual behaviors, erotic identities, constructions of gender, forms of knowledge, regimes of enunciation, logics of representation, modes of self-constitution, and practices of community—for restructuring, that is, the relations among power, truth, and desire."

I believe that, in a society where we are not stigmatized for our sex and gender preferences, we could develop multifarious sex and gender presentations—liberating everyone and oppressing no one.

8.

It is the law of my own voice I shall investigate, Frank O'Hara proclaims in a poem of 1970, "Homosexuality," which continues:

> *I start like ice, my finger to my ear, my ear*
> *to my heart*

… in this posture—ear to heart—ice in voice, I continue.

MY TATTOOS
On Madonna

One's on my left shoulder blade, the second on my right inner-bicep, and the third on my chest near my heart—each tattoo, a sequence of three Hebrew letters:

1) *aleph, lamed, daled*
2) *kaf, hey, tav*
3) *nun, lamed, kaf*

"What do they say?" I'm asked time after time.

"They don't translate," I'll bashfully answer and elaborate that in Jewish mysticism—or, in Kabbalah—they're symbolic, protective, intended to ward off bad luck. I'll explain, "I was a teenager."

*

I was a teenager in the early 2000s, when Madonna was avidly advocating the creeds of the Kabbalah Centre, a nonprofit organization established in 1984 by Karen and Philip Berg. Among numerous displays of devotion to Kabbalah, Madonna (and I) wore a bracelet of red yarn, which supposedly had been wrapped around Rachel's Tomb in the West Bank, thereby infused with—and so, providing for the wearer—the protection that the biblical Rachel provided for her children. Sold by the Kabbalah Centre, the red string should be knotted seven times on the left wrist ("the receiving side of the body and soul," reads the packaging), tied by a loved one who recites the Ben Porat Prayer in Hebrew, while visualizing, from right to left, aleph, lamed, and daled:

The Kabbalah Centre identifies seventy-two of these combinations, each purported to evoke supernatural energies for various specific purposes, such as victory over addiction, the ability to speak the right words, or finding one's soulmate.

My tattoos:
1) banish the evil eye
2) deflect negativity
3) eradicate illness

*

Kabbalah entered my consciousness at age eleven, via an episode of *The X-Files* titled "Kaddish" that aired February 16, 1997. Mulder believes a golem—an inhuman creature brought to life from mud or clay—has avenged the death of a Hasidic person killed by neo-Nazis. Mulder and Scully find the Hasidic person's body buried with a self-immolating book on mystical Judaism, and they consult a Jewish scholar who introduces the supernatural concept of Kabbalah. My mother mentioned the episode to my aunt, the most religious person in our family, and my aunt revealed that she considered Kabbalah to be taboo. Such a queer, illicit quality provoked my curiosity.

The study of Kabbalah had been restricted to married men over forty for many centuries (until 1969, according to the Kabbalah Centre, when the Bergs claim to have opened it for observation in popular culture), and the Kabbalistic doctrine has been long obfuscated by misinformation and occluded by occultism.

(This is also true of tattoos. I grew up believing that tattooed bodies can't receive burial in Jewish cemeteries—a common misconception based on this passage in Leviticus, which forbids tattooing in general: "Ye shall not make any cuttings in your flesh for the dead, nor print any marks upon you." While a small number of Jewish burial societies adhere to this prohibition, it isn't a standard practice.)

Already prone to magical thinking, I was entrenched in mysticisms—and soon to be diagnosed with obsessive-compulsive disorder. Terrified of "evil" numbers, I glorified "good" numbers, and I believed that certain thoughts or actions had the power to manifest desired or undesired outcomes. I bought a stack of New Age books on Kabbalah at Mirabai of Woodstock—but found the information too opaque and lackluster. Then, nearly a decade later, the Kabbalah Centre started publishing commercially oriented spirituality titles, which, despite being riddled with falsehoods and oversimplifications, rendered the fundamental ideas of Kabbalah with newfangled glamor and accessibility for people around the world, including Madonna and me.

*

Harold Bloom's *Kabbalah and Criticism* pragmatically demystifies Kabbalistic evolution, depicting Kabbalah's foundational texts as works of poetic literary criticism on the Torah.

Bloom reads Gershom Scholem's definitive history, *Kabbalah*, to reveal the roots of the tradition—and the term *kabbalah* roughly translates in English as "tradition," Bloom conveys, "in the particular sense of 'reception.'"

Gershom Scholem traces Kabbalah's origins to the influence of writings by Jewish mystics who, circa 100 BCE to 1000 CE, recorded visions of encounters with the universal creator, whose superhuman form is described in hallucinatory detail: "They enumerate the fantastic measurements of parts of the head as well as some of the limbs. They also transmit 'the secret names' of these limbs, all of them unintelligible letter combinations." The emerging Kabbalistic doctrine would build upon this generative power transmitted through sequences of unintelligible letter combinations.

The earliest document ascribed to Kabbalah, *Sefer Yezirah* ("The Book of Creation"), was composed in Palestine sometime during the third to sixth century CE, according to Scholem, by "a devout Jew with leanings toward mysticism"—though its authorship is often dated earlier and even attributed to Abraham. The author of *Sefer Yezirah* believed, as Scholem describes: "From the primal air God created, or 'engraved' upon it, the 22 letters" of the Hebrew alphabet. To Scholem, *Sefer Yezirah* conveyed that "the world-process is essentially a linguistic one, based on the unlimited combinations of the letters." Thus, the secret names' generative power assembles the Kabbalist's entire worldview.

To Bloom, *Sefer Yezirah* offers "no literary or spiritual value, but historically it is the true origin of Kabbalah" because it blueprints the Sefirot: "the divine emanations by which all reality is structured." (More on the Sefirot soon.) Bloom finds more value in the second-most foundational Kabbalistic text, *Sefer ha-Zohar* ("The Book of Splendor"), commonly referred to as the *Zohar*—a collection of manuscripts written in Aramaic that Scholem attributed to Moses de León, who wrote in Guadalajara circa 1280.

In the Kabbalah Centre's national bestseller *The Power of Kabbalah* (which Madonna blurbed: "No hocus-pocus here. Nothing to do with religious dogma, the ideas in this book are earth-shattering and yet so simple"), Yehuda Berg asserts that the *Zohar* was written during the second century, then discovered by Moses de León circa 1270—this, one of several discrepancies touted by the Kabbalah Centre.

The *Zohar* largely comprises lyrical exposition of the Torah: riddles and anecdotes that encourage a modern approach to deciphering an ancient text. Bloom explains: "The *Zohar* is organized as an apparent commentary upon Scripture, just as much as the later Kabbalah is organized as an apparent commentary upon the *Zohar*." Scholem underlines the *Zohar*'s emphasis on observing the Ten Commandments in order to safeguard the collective fate of the Jewish faith and community, and he highlights the Sefirot, a structure of metaphysical planes that radiate out from the heavens to the human realm—providing, in Bloom, "an immutable knowledge of a final reality that stands behind our world of appearances"—a channel of direct connection with the creator and, at the same time, a series of partitions that obstruct the human realm from eternal light: the light that results from a Big Bang-like event, wherefrom existence emanates. Scholem locates this same eternal light within the sacred secret names.

Over the next two centuries, Kabbalistic literature proliferated—particularly rabbinical commentary on the *Zohar*—and especially in Spain, where philosophy, sympathetic magic, and meditation were combined to attempt what Scholem notes as "return through mystic communion to [the] original source." Following the penultimate turning point in Kabbalistic history—the expulsion of the Jewish people, who included my mother's mother's ancestors, from Spain in 1492—Scholem notices that Kabbalah aimed at a new objective: a messianic "journey toward redemption." Around 1530, in Palestine, Isaac Luria emerged as the last major Kabbalistic innovator, appearing in Scholem as a charismatic messiah-figure to the recently dispersed Jewish people. Among his offerings: "exercises in meditation based on mental concentration on the combinations of Sacred Names."

Advanced by Luria's teachings, what had been conceived, in Bloom, as a "rhetorical series of techniques for opening Scripture" matured into "a fresh and vital new religious impulse, in a precarious and even catastrophic time of troubles." In Bloom, "Before Luria, all of Kabbalah saw creation as a progressive process, moving in one direction always, emanating out from God... In Luria, creation is a startlingly regressive process, one in which an abyss can separate any one stage from another, and in which catastrophe is always a central event."

After Luria, Kabbalistic doctrine became fanatically focused on how to live a good life despite the omnipresence of evil: a force that weighs down humanity, hindering transcendence. And transcendence—to contact the source of the eternal light of the Sefirot—would be humanity's salvation.

Kabbalistic methods of organizing life by analyzing literature laid the groundwork for Hasidic Judaism in the eighteenth century and Orthodox Judaism in the nineteenth, while Kabbalah's façade also became scaffolded by more non-Jewish traditions and superstitions across time. Abstracting Kabbalistic history and intention, the Kabbalah Centre embellished the tradition's mystic tendencies and fashioned a franchise of self-help coping mechanisms for confronting evil in the twentieth century.

Bloom concludes: "In its degeneracy, Kabbalah has sought vainly for a magical power over nature, but in its glory it sought, and found, a power of the mind over the universe of death."

*

Madonna's music entered my consciousness at age six. In 1992, she sang "This Used to Be My Playground" for the closing credits of the film *A League of Their Own*—a fictionalization of the real-life 1950s All American Girls Professional Baseball League—in which she also costars, and which was partially filmed (and so boastfully popular) in my hometown, Cooperstown, New York. Faintly aware of Madonna before then, her scandalous reputation for radical sensuality had intimidated me. The same year *A League of Their Own* opened in theaters, Madonna released her fifth LP, *Erotica*, and published an X-rated coffee-table book entitled *Sex* (sold shrink-wrapped and kept behind the checkout counter at my local Waldenbooks). Even in the film, one of her central scenes features her character teaching an illiterate teammate to read by sounding out sentences from a so-called sleaze novel. Still terrified by my repressed queerness, I subconsciously aspired to be the chaste, stern type portrayed by Geena Davis's character.

But in 1996, I played, rewound, and replayed my double-cassette of the *Evita* film soundtrack until the tapes wore thin and then severed, and I pirated the movie on a blank VHS during a weekend of free HBO. Here, Madonna's image altered dramatically: as Eva Duarte de Perón, First Lady of Argentina and polarizing candidate for the country's vice presidency—who rose from actress and model to advocate for labor rights and women's suffrage—dubbed "Spiritual Leader of the Nation" by Argentine National Congress, deceased at thirty-three, and depicted as coquettish starlet turned stalwart politician by a thirty-seven-year-old polarizing pop star. My beloved fifth-grade teacher listened to Madonna's *Evita* on a CD player while the students left the classroom for lunch and recess; I suspect her private enjoyment of that music incited my interest.

My era of hardcore Madonna fandom was fully underway by 1998—one year after that Kabbalistic *X-Files* episode—when she released the music video for "Frozen" from *Ray of Light*. With her slender face draped by long, straight, black hair (uncannily resembling my mother's slender face and long, straight, black hair)—her hands inked with henna, the Sanskrit symbol for *om* drawn on her palm—the song's content and the video's aesthetics unmistakably reveal Madonna's existential inquiry. I converted. I sketched lines of henna on my hands and scribbled the symbol for *om* on my notebooks. Almost thirteen, I was one year shy of outwardly admitting my queerness.

*

Madonna's involvement with the Kabbalah Centre commenced around 1996, at the age of thirty-eight, the year she delivered her firstborn. Although 1998's *Ray of Light* conveyed notions more Buddhist than Kabbalist, it conspicuously deviated from the hedonistic debauchery that dominated the inaugural decade of her career.

I believe her campaign for Kabbalah reached crowning visibility with the release of her music video for "Die Another Day" (theme song to the eponymous James Bond film) in 2002. The video's main narrative features Madonna in custody—dirty; bloody; blond hair chopped at the jawline; wearing black slacks, black bra, and white tank top; outer right bicep tattooed with three Hebrew characters: lamed, aleph, and vav—as two executioners drag her down a hallway and then strap her to an electric chair. At the video's end, the outlines of lamed, aleph, and vav burn into the back panel of the empty chair as Madonna escapes the facility.

According to *The 72 Names of God*, another national bestseller for the Kabbalah Centre by Yehuda Berg, this letter arrangement—the only one of the seventy-two that's assigned dual functions—facilitates both "banishing the remnants of evil" and "great escape": the latter illustrated by comparison to fleeing the "prison" of the ego.

"Kabbalah says the Bible is a complete code," Berg imparts. "It's a cryptogram. When this Biblical code is cracked, something wonderful happens: awesome spiritual forces are suddenly released into our souls and discharged into the world at large." By means of the "most powerful and most ancient technology" of Berg's seventy-two names, each letter sequence "operates much like a cable transmitting various blends of energy into our physical world." Meditating on "their unique shapes" and "the patterns expressed in their lines and curves" imbues you with their power: "you stop your reflexive egocentric impulses and unleash the proactive will of your soul." You activate each Name by simply seeing it. You look, and "spiritual Light of unimaginable force and brilliance is ignited." Here, the Kabbalah Centre most faithfully recreates the original Kabbalistic intention: to engage with texts and letter combinations as conduits for accessing the eternal light of the Sefirot.

Interviewing Madonna about Kabbalah in 2002, Larry King asked, "What attracted you to it?"

> MADONNA: I was looking for something. I mean, I'd begun practicing yoga and, you know, I was looking for the answers—to life. Why am I here? What am I doing here? What is my purpose? How do I fit in to the big picture? I know there's more to life than making lots of money and being successful. And even getting married and having a family, you know—where does it go? What is the point? What is the point of my journey and everybody else's journey?
>
> LARRY KING: What's it all mean.

MADONNA: What's it all mean? And why is there so much chaos in the world? And is this just the way it goes? You know, and I wanted to know the answers.

Yehuda Berg's *The Red String Book* (companion to the package of red yarn), a pocket-size manual published by the Kabbalah Centre, vaunts:

> Kabbalah unravels all the mysteries of the universe. In the process, it reveals the spiritual and physical laws that govern both the universe and the human soul... It offers practical tools with which to effect authentic change in your life. It creates order out of chaos. And as if that weren't enough, Kabbalah answers the ultimate question of human existence: *Why are we here on this earth?*

In the end, the Kabbalah Centre's tactile rituals of concentration and distraction—its enigmas, its illusions of control—can assist in diverting a person's energy away from chaos. Belief in the seventy-two names and the red string, for instance, lends some moral support in conquering the evils of insecurity and impermanence. After all—before all—*The Red String Book* assures us, we chose existence over nonbeing. Why? We wanted—like our creator—to enact the ecstasy of creation.

*

August 26, 2001—age fifteen (one year after declaring my queerness)—at my mother's father's house in Pomona, New York, I watched HBO's live broadcast of Madonna's Drowned World Tour performance at the Palace of Auburn Hills in Michigan (which neighbors Madonna's hometown, Rochester Hills). Svelte and self-assured, she exhibited such contentment in her Pilates-sculpted body, she tantalized an appetite for contentment in my own fleshy physique. The next night, I binged and purged for the first time in an ensuing decade of grueling control over my weight and shape through bouts of bulimia and anorexia—as well as an obsession with yoga, instigated by Madonna's yoga practice. In a yearbook portrait from 2002, I'm skeletal—spectral—my eyes bulge from sunken sockets, my smile beams broader than the width of my pallid face. I remember the sensation of being svelte, self-assured, so content I could've expired. Having modeled my values on Madonna's latest lifestyle appropriations, I'd created myself in her image.

*

Madonna's existential inquiry emerged in her music several years before entering mass-media spectacle. I believe it became markedly overt near the end of 1994's *Bedtime Stories*.

Throughout the penultimate track, "Bedtime Story" (cowritten by Björk and so, suffused with Björk's gravitas), the narrator takes a vow of silence.

> *Words are useless*
> *Especially sentences*
> *They don't stand for anything...*

The tone and subject matter of *Ray of Light*, Madonna's subsequent studio album, follows a natural progression from "Bedtime Story"— though she spent those intervening years, 1996 to 1998, filming and promoting *Evita*, for which she'd recorded the score in 1995.

Incidentally, the original 1970s *Evita* musical soundtrack was forbidden in the house of my mother's mother—owing to the real-life Peróns' alleged allegiance with the Nazis hiding in Argentina. While my mother's mother—once, the most religious person in our family—was a staunch Zionist, I am staunchly opposed to Zionism. Madonna's position appears to be ambivalent; while she has repeatedly traveled to Israeli-occupied Kabbalistic sites such as Rachel's

Tomb in the West Bank, her 2019 Eurovision performance in Tel Aviv featured Palestinian flags onstage.

Having played Eva Perón from adolescence to death—succeeded, in reality, by pregnancy with her firstborn—Madonna encountered a resurgence of her desire for spiritual guidance. *Evita*'s finale, "Lament," conveys Eva's departing words.

> *I saw the lights, and I was on my way*
> *And how I lived, how they shone*
> *But how soon the lights were gone...*

"Lament" appeared on the set-list for Madonna's 2004 Re-Invention Tour, and the tour's documentary film, *I'm Going to Tell You a Secret*, contains footage of it; she sings (her chiseled torso corseted in a red-and-white-striped circus-style bodice; her striated thighs stretching against sheer-black, knee-length leggings, her bulbous calves bulging above crimson stilettos), seated on an electric chair. A colossal set piece studded with lightbulbs—forming the shapes of aleph, lamed, and daled—blinks on and off behind her.

*

After remission from eating disorders in my late teens (excluding a few relapse episodes in my early twenties)—through talk therapy, medication, and painstaking willpower—Madonna's influence found another outlet on my body.

The first tattoo was done by Pat, at Pat's Tatts in Kingston, New York, the summer following graduation from high school—aleph, lamed, daled: on my left shoulder—for protection from evil.

The second tattoo, one year later—kaf, hey, tav: on my right arm, to deflect negative energy—was done in a parlor near my mother's house in Oneonta, New York, by a person whose face, arms, and legs were swathed with solid, greenish blue-black banners and blocks that masked previous tattoos of neo-Nazi iconography.

The third and last tattoo was done one year after the second, at 33 Saint Mark's Place, the building where my mother's father's parents raised their family—nun, lamed, kaf: on my chest over my heart— for good health.

Armoring myself in unintelligible letter combinations—both sacred and profane: talismanic shields, ultimately meant to prevent premature death, etched into my skin (*Touch me, I'm dying*, Madonna implores on *Ray of Light*'s "Skin")—I'm permanently ornamented with the indelible emblems of my desire for spiritual guidance.

*

Kim Gordon's memoir, *Girl in a Band*, muses on Madonna in the 1980s Manhattan music scene: "Her voice wasn't strong, and she wasn't an obvious diva." Gordon—whose tough voice enchants me—continued: "She had a knack for knowing how to entertain," and "she seemed joyful, celebrating her own body," and "you could feel how happy she was inhabiting that body."

Madonna's voice didn't induce my decade of idolatry, but I was mesmerized by how zealously she dwelled in her body. I'd bow at her feet until 2005's *Confessions on a Dance Floor*, but I haven't listened to a single album since the live CD/DVD of *The Confessions Tour*: the tour I finally attended, at the Hartford Civic Center in Connecticut, in June 2006, with one of my aunts and one of my cousins. That year, Madonna fell out of vogue with the Kabbalah Centre, owing to financial concerns around her joint charity foundation with the Bergs, and then the Kabbalah Centre fell from grace in 2011, under investigation by the IRS and charged with a sexual harassment lawsuit by a former student. Disconnected from Kabbalah, Madonna's image has reverted to the Catholic iconoclast of *Like a*

Prayer—motivated more by rebellious extroversion than by existential insight or spiritual profundity.

*

Nowadays, I keep fond acquaintance and embarrassed distance from Madonna's music as well as my tattoos. From time to time, someone will insist on trying to translate the Hebrew—despite my insistence that it's not meant to be read literally—as I conceal the ink with my hands and steer the conversation elsewhere. But occasionally, I'll receive a knowing nod or wink of kinship—some recognition of a shared language, some acknowledgment of an incredible need to believe—from a fellow reformed disciple of Madonna's Kabbalah.

MASSAGE THE HISTORY
On Kim Gordon

1. THE SONIC YOUTH

On September 7, 2013, Manhattan's White Columns gallery opened an exhibition of visual art by Kim Gordon. The first survey of her ongoing practice, it gathered paintings—hand-lettered names of broken-up bands ("Weak Sister") and witticisms ("Why are you making music like that?")—alongside sculpture (tree branches encrusted in glitter, denim skirts slathered in acrylic), with selections of video, text, and sound spanning more than thirty years of songwriting and performance. The unspoken centerpiece, a new work: a stiff canvas crumpled on the floor—a pile resembling a queen-size comforter kicked off the mattress during sex or sleep—ebony words applied in dripping, misshapen font, indecipherable because scrunched. A nearby plaque told its title: *The Sonic Youth*.

2. SONIC NURSE

I'm a born-again fan of Sonic Youth. I didn't learn how to admire their music until 2012, a year after the band dissolved. Now, more than a decade since the release of their final album, *The Eternal*, my reverence—especially for the complex texture of Kim Gordon's voice—verges on evangelical.

At the pinnacle of adolescence, age sixteen, my obsessive-compulsive disorder receded into relative latency, and for several years I gained a stronger sense of security and agency. Around 2010, in my early twenties, the infidelity of a new love interest and the betrayal of an old friend triggered my OCD to relapse. In 2012, my symptoms had become worse than ever before, further triggered by the infidelity of my new romantic partner and the emotional abuse inflicted by my new employers. I'd recently been fired from an underpaid entry-level position in publishing, then hired by another publisher for an underpaid entry-level position. Earning a salary far below the bare minimum required by New York City's living expenses, I sold my books to secondhand bookstores at the end of every month in order to pay rent. Hunger burned in my gut, daily, owing to what I called a "scarcity diet," consisting mainly of coffee, bread, and peanut butter. Four times in four years, I moved out of one overpriced apartment into the next. I could've left the city, could've returned to my mother's house and my conservative, rural hometown: a fate—for a queer person living in a queer epicenter—like death. Debilitating anxieties of death, loss, abandonment, and uncertainty stalked my every thought and action. In the throes of this distress, I sought some way to sublimate such persistent dread of pain and danger.

Kim Gordon, Thurston Moore, and Lee Ranaldo—all vocalists and guitarists—had their inaugural performance as Sonic Youth in June 1981, at White Columns (the gallery then located on Spring Street). In 1982, they released a self-titled debut EP, with drummer Richard Edson, and two subsequent LPs—*Confusion Is Sex* (1983) and *Bad Moon Rising* (1985)—with drummer Bob Bert. The third LP, *EVOL* (1986), premiered drummer Steve Shelley, who became the fourth core member. Their following twelve LPs, numerous side projects, and collaborations are unanimously considered unclassifiable; they're notorious for mistreating their instruments (shoving screwdrivers and steel files between guitar strings, bashing a maraca on the snare and cymbals) to unearth unprecedented noise.

I waded for years before I could fathom this sound. I'd started listening in 2004: "Unmade Bed"—the second track from their then-latest album, *Sonic Nurse*—engulfed me at eighteen. It's one of their more palatable songs. Thurston's singing is mellow, fluent; the lengthy instrumental bridge never goes totally over the edge into that free-fall of guttural guitars and chaotic drums for which they're either loved or loathed. "Unmade Bed" floated on the rising tide of a surging flood that Sonic Youth would eventually plummet me within: a definitive encounter with *the sublime*.

3. THE SUBLIME

Edmund Burke's *A Philosophical Enquiry into the Origin of Our Ideas of the Sublime and Beautiful* says: "Whatever is fitted in any sort to excite the ideas of pain, and danger... whatever is in any sort terrible, or is conversant about terrible objects, or operates in a manner analogous to terror, is a source of the *sublime*; that is, it is productive of the strongest emotion which the mind is capable of feeling."

If we say something's sublime, I think we often do intend to evoke *the strongest emotion the mind is capable of feeling*, but I think we rarely intend to evoke *pain and danger*.

Burke recognized that pain and danger are not themselves sublime. The real sublime, he specifies, lies in "the sensation which accompanies the removal of pain or danger," which he called *delight*. "When danger or pain press too nearly, they are incapable of giving any delight, and are simply terrible; but at certain distances, and with certain modifications, they may be, and they are delightful."

If something's truly sublime, it must push you thrush against mortality—terrifying you through dread of unavoidable death—before pulling you back into the awful delight of survival.

4. KIM'S CHORDS

At its most severe, Sonic Youth's sound aggresses—it pounds and wails—it's indeed painful for a sensitive listener. Even at its most serene, critics have repeatedly described their sound as *ominous*, and that's accurate: 99 percent of the songs could background a scene in a horror film. And in fact, they did compose and record the score for a French horror film, *Simon Werner a Disparu*—titled *Lights Out* in the US.

But I delight in listening *because* of that dangerous tenor: their tendency to swerve from tonal optimism to droll nihilism in a millisecond. Sonic Youth soundtracks the impending doom that constantly haunts me; it helps me embrace uncertainty.

You can hear this characteristic in an outtake from the *Sonic Nurse* sessions, an instrumental tune titled "Kim's Chords," reminiscent of driving out of LA into Malibu on a blue-sky day, for three-minutes-twenty-two seconds—until suddenly the car skids off the Pacific Coast Highway, smacks into the ocean, combusts, then sinks for three more minutes.

Kim (born in California) writes in her memoir, *Girl in a Band*: "California is a place of death, a place people are drawn to because they don't realize deep down they're actually afraid of what they want. It's new, and they're escaping their histories while at the same time moving headlong toward their own extinctions. Desire and death are all mixed up with the thrill and the risk of the unknown."

5. THAT OCEANIC FEELING

Burke's sublime feels kindred to what Sigmund Freud deemed *that oceanic feeling*. The French writer Romain Rolland alluded to it in his 1927 correspondence with Freud—*"the sensation of the 'eternal'* (which may very well not be eternal, but simply without perceptible limits, and in that way oceanic)"—and Freud expanded on the concept in *Civilization and Its Discontents*.

Further elucidated by Julia Kristeva in *This Incredible Need to Believe*, that oceanic feeling is "the intimate union of the ego with the surrounding world, felt as an absolute certainty of satisfaction, security, as well as loss of our self to what surrounds and contains us..." Though Kristeva maintains Freud's belief that this feeling is "unshareable," I think it's vaguely comparable to the wanderlust prompted by watching an aircraft coast across the skyline—imagine me, writing this on an overcast midwinter afternoon in a freezing apartment in Park Slope, Brooklyn, yearning for the sun above Big Sur—and suddenly that thrill of risk flows through, tempting me to get a plane ticket and go (but then I remember that I can't afford it). That oceanic feeling is this homesickness, lacking origin and cure.

Another facet of the oceanic feeling: desire for "losing the boundaries of the self... into the pain-and-joy of becoming fluid, of liquefying oneself *to be other*." Imagine beholding the ocean from the cliffs of the Pacific Coast Highway, overcome with the desire to submerge your body in that water. You can hear this melancholic longing in "The Diamond Sea"—the nineteen-minute closing track on Sonic Youth's *Washing Machine* (1995)—at the crest of its extended, formless, instrumental bridge, the guitar overtones conjure sunlight strafing the inmost curl of a breaking tidal wave: a searing sound, shrill as a newborn shrieking to go back inside the womb.

"Positive and negative, joy and extreme pain, together or in alteration. This brew of plenitude and sensory emptying crushes the body and exiles it... the psyche is in its turn annihilated, beyond the self..." (Kristeva).

I seek that kind of sublime all the time: to merge with sound by any tangible means—I wear my *Washing Machine* T-shirt and play "Washing Machine" on laundry day—to remember the demise that is my only destiny, relieved I've eluded it for now. I wrote this—sublimating my suffering into representation—to temporarily exit my anxiety and still exist.

6. THE ETERNAL

Sonic Youth and *The Eternal* technically function as the first and last entries in the band's repertoire of studio albums—and both incidentally so. Comprised of five songs and running twenty-four minutes, the self-titled EP was their debut de facto, prefiguring their earliest LP, *Confusion Is Sex*. *The Eternal* wasn't meant to be their terminal LP upon release by Matador in June 2009—the band continued touring and recording until an abrupt split two years later, coinciding with Kim and Thurston's divorce. In January 2011, their homegrown label Sonic Youth Recordings (founded in 1996) released its ninth installment: the original soundtrack for that French horror film—instrument-only tracks in the vein of "Kim's Chords"—which *Pitchfork* predicted were "blueprints for a future Sonic Youth album." Five months later, May 2011, Thurston hinted to *NME* about their plans to record new material. However, in October, Matador announced the band's indefinite hiatus. The next month, on November 14, they played their final show in São Paulo.

7. I DREAMED I DREAM

"The Burning Spear"—the opening track on Sonic Youth's debut EP—is twenty-eight words long. Thurston's birth-cry:

I'm not afraid to say I'm scared
In my bed I'm deep in prayer.
I trust the speed, I love the fear
The music comes, the burning spear.

Menacingly, the guitars squeal, the bass and drums sprint—a drug-fueled high-speed police-chase around Alphabet City. From the get-go, Sonic Youth confronted danger head-on: They *love* the fear.

"Fear being an apprehension of pain or death," Burke declared.

Exposure and response prevention (ERP), a form of cognitive behavioral therapy developed for the treatment of OCD, involves learning how to love fear. The apprehension of pain and death can be mitigated through confronting and accepting its inevitability; intentional exposure to feared thoughts and actions can gradually retrain the brain and prevent obsessive-compulsive responses. When I wrote this, I was three years out of my first ERP treatment, two years away from my second ERP treatment, and six years into my practice of self-soothing through plumbing the depths of Sonic Youth's discography.

"I Dreamed I Dream" (track two on their debut EP) launches with the speedy pulse of the bass accompanied by a ticking drum—twelve seconds—then the guitars join. Tension upon tension (sneaky, prowling), they've outrun the police-chase of "The Burning Spear" and they're laying low in Tompkins Square Park.

Now, Kim Gordon doesn't sing—she speaks—her opening lines in Sonic Youth's catalog: *Look before you leap, OK*, shimmers her crystalline pitch.

Here, the announcement of a radical, stalwart voice—the voice that'll ask, in 1990, on *Goo*'s "Kool Thing": *Are you gonna liberate us girls from male, white, corporate oppression?*

Kim's capable of conventional singing—Sonic Youth's penultimate LP, *Rather Ripped* (2006), presents her vocals at peak approachability—nevertheless, she primarily opts for tones that're lovely ugly: phlegmatic, thick-tongued lilts and hoarse, throaty moans. "Talk Normal" implores one of her text paintings, as if mocking potential criticism for this proclivity.

"She has a distinctly physical response to language," writes Hilton Als, in Kim's 2009 monograph of impressionistic watercolor portraits, *Performing/Guzzling.* "Her speech, suffused with pauses and directness, quiet reflection and near novelistic sense of detail and memory for conversation, is the aural corollary to her visual work, which swims in the language and non-language of what she sees... eyes looking at her as she performs, faces she and we half remember, as though recalled from a collective, half-forgotten dream."

8. INFINITY

"Another source of the sublime, is *infinity*," Burke decreed. "Infinity has a tendency to fill the mind with that sort of delightful horror, which is the most genuine effect, and the truest test of the sublime."

I've been long drawn to the mathematical symbol for infinity—the *lemniscate*:

That oceanic feeling encompasses the ongoingness demonstrated by this figure: the past as immeasurable as the future—the present moment recoils, doubles back on itself—nonbeing endlessly extending behind us and ahead. We drift, dead center in these roiling high seas.

Burke noted that "madmen" in thrall to infinitude "remain whole days and nights, sometimes whole years, in the constant repetition of some remark, some complaint, or song; which having struck powerfully on their disordered imagination, in the beginning of their frenzy, every repetition reinforces it with new strength…"

"I Dreamed I Dream" contains a phrase that recurs in 2009's "Massage the History": *All the money's gone.* In the former, age twenty-nine, Kim reiterates: *All the money's gone*; in the latter, twenty-seven years later, she goes on to warble: *But it was never here.*

One of the scariest durations of my early adulthood transpired while I was being mistreated at work and distrustful of my partner, saddled with mounting credit card debt and a declining bank account balance—all my money almost gone (and never there in the first place).

I've kept a playlist on my iPhone—only "I Dreamed I Dream" and "Massage the History"—and when set on shuffle, as soon as one stops, the other starts. Listening to the two on loop, I make this little infinity; holding a beginning in my left hand and an ending in my right, I massage their history.

9. THE OTHER SIDE

The swansong of *The Eternal* commences with ambient glistening for six seconds, then the bass and drums cruise in, flirting for sixteen seconds. Thurston enters with a toothsome lick on acoustic guitar, mimicking Kim's melody, which will start at one-minute-forty-five seconds, when she croons:

> *Oil dripping on my head*
> *Let's go back to bed.*

Back to the unmade bed of "The Burning Spear"—in youth, in prayer, in love with fear?

Kim proceeds in hushed headvoice. As her vocals fade out, the instruments stall, slipping onto a suspenseful plateau, then incrementally build back to a tempestuous pitch—shattering guitars and slamming drums—it sounds like heavy metal: the cellar door of the subconscious blasted open.

"Something's really at stake in this performance," Ben Ratliff wrote in *The New York Times*. "[Kim sings] 'Come with me to the other side / Not everyone makes it out alive.' There's some trick emotion here, in the singing and the music, something unsettled and uncertain."

It's that oceanic feeling crashing down again, needing to reach its source, wanting to take you home.

10. BODY/HEAD

"Massage the History" ends on the word *neck*—its last line: *I want you to suck my neck*.

According to the liner notes, it technically ends on *suck*:

> *I want you to suck my neck.*
> *Suck.*

To my ear, Kim utters half of suck—"suh"—upholding *neck* as the full departing word.

Massaging this fact enhances the inevitability of Kim's next venture. After Sonic Youth's dispersal, her next project was a duo with guitarist Bill Nace called Body/Head. And what's between the head and the rest of the body? The neck.

Coming Apart, their debut LP—recorded in December 2012, released by Matador in September 2013—comprises ten phantasmagoric songs: sixty-eight minutes of distended strumming and gaunt vocal riffs. Through Body/Head, Kim's enunciation—visceral mixture of rapture and torture—approaches a primal scream. Tellingly, she recounts in *Girl in a Band* that when coming of age, she visited the home of Arthur Janov—in her words, "the creator of the primal scream, a therapy technique that was supposed to return you to your birth trauma experience and release you by encouraging screaming and other vocal disinhibitions."

Ten miniscule films correspond to the pieces of *Coming Apart*; in each, one slight gesture replays in slow motion for the song's entirety. The film for "Can't Help You"—the album's most amicable track—features Louise Erdman, Kim's niece, miming Kim's noise-band-name-painting technique: A pair of pantyhose, soaked in paint and then lashed against the canvas, creates the lines of every letter.

11. MURDERED OUT

Body/Head aside, Kim's music continued infusing more mainstream channels with the (life-affirming) essence of pain and danger.

- In June 2015, her track for the Converse sneaker-company's compilation *CONS EP VOL. III* began streaming: "Slow Boy"—a collaboration with Dinosaur Jr.'s guitar prodigy, J Mascis. At one-minute-thirty-six-seconds, and again at two-minutes-fifty-seconds, Kim's horrific wail trails off to an identical note by J's guitar, which then propels the phrase faster, higher than any human range: a sort of sublimation.

- In August 2015, Peaches released "Close Up," a single featuring Kim; in it, she rasps: *Look to the right, lemme get a close-up*—her timbre intimidating, macabre.

- In March 2016, she and surf-pro Alex Knost put out a self-titled EP as Glitterbust—fifty-two minutes of libidinous droning, austere guitar, seldom drum, and intermittent poetic recitation—five hyper-erotic, angst-ridden tracks, delighting in their foreboding.

Then, in September 2016, Matador released a chilling single—
"Murdered Out"—the first-ever track credited to Kim Gordon
by name alone. Cloaked in heavy reverb, her speak-singing thrusts
the hook—*black matte spray*—to grungy dance-club drumming.
Interviewed by NPR, Kim explained that to murder out a car—to
coat it in matte-black spray paint—erases the logo, its corporate
identification: "It's almost like a peaceful resistance. It's denying that
we're part of the culture, that we're not going to fit in. We're making
our own kind of anti-status symbol, in our own language that's kind
of subliminal."

Today, Body/Head endures as Kim's preferred creative endeavor.
Two months after "Murdered Out" debuted, Body/Head released a
recording of their forty-minute set from March 2014 at the Big Ears
Festival in Knoxville, Tennessee. Its cover adorned with a seascape
by Raymond Pettibon, the live album is named *No Waves*.*

12. TEEN AGE RIOT

"Even though Sonic Youth is associated with it, it would be wrong
to call us No Wave. We just built something out of it," Kim asserts
in *Girl in a Band*. "When I saw and heard No Wave bands, some
equation in my head and body pieced together instantly. A phantom *thing* had been missing from my life and here it was, finally,
unconventional, personal but at the same time not, and confron-
tational. What's more, every No Wave gig felt precarious, a rush, a
cheek-burn, since you knew the band onstage could break up at any
moment."

On November 14, 2011—at an outdoor stage in São Paulo—Sonic
Youth played their final show. You can see professional video

---

* After I wrote this, *No Waves* was followed by Body/Head's studio LP, *The Switch*, in July
2018. In October 2019, Kim released a debut solo LP, *No Home Record*, under her full name
alone. And then, Body/Head dropped an EP, *Come On*, in May 2023.

footage on YouTube, intensely imbued with this threat of imminent termination that Kim describes. Go, hear her quaver the set-opener, "Brave Men Run (In My Family)"—here, her utterance is sibylline, her intonations diamond-cut, excavated from the diaphragm, scraping the throat on the way out of her gritted teeth. Listening, I'm awash in the pain and joy of approaching danger. It's *astonishing*. "Astonishment is that state of the soul, in which all its motions are suspended, with some degree of horror," Burke concluded: "The effect of the sublime in the highest degree…"

The mood lifts for "Sacred Trickster" (*The Eternal*'s opening track), Sonic Youth's ars poetica; the chorus—*Getting dizzy, sitting around, Sacred Trickster and a no-tech sound*—conclusively categorizes their style, their own invention: "no-tech." *What's it like to be a girl in a band?* Kim drawls, bouncing and swaying, wearing a vermillion box-cut dress. But that's the eye of the storm. By the time they play "'Cross the Breeze," it's drenched in that oceanic feeling, and not just because when the camera pans out—beyond the crowd of thousands and thousands of people—you can see twilight on the South Atlantic in the distance: Near the end of its gut-wrenching prolonged outro, Thurston knocks his knuckles and fingertips on the back of the fret, convulsing, then he rocks back and forth, plucking the strings' taut ends, possessed. Lee plays with the effects pedals to generate a wistful underwater whir. Drumming the intro to their next song—"Schizophrenia"—Steve, whose eyes usually flicker in frenetic delight, appears to scarcely resist sobbing.

"Teen Age Riot"—their hymn to youth, their anthem for anarchy— closes the set (nostalgic, euphoric), followed by seven minutes of apocalyptic noise improvisation, concluding shortly after Kim starts whipping the electrical cords from the outlets, striding offstage.

Now—the São Paulo video over—I put on the seventy-five-minute concert footage of April 4, 1996, at Rockpalast in Dusseldorf, Germany.

I watch the set-opener—"Teen Age Riot"—and then press pause.

Here, now, they are—and I am (you can be, too)—invincible, still halfway through their career together, at an eternal pinnacle of adolescence.

COULD WE

On Cat Power

I'm obsessed with bootlegs of Cat Power concerts. I've saved more than forty hours of amateur and professional recordings on my hard drive, and I've spent probably thousands of hours listening. It's medicinal, meditative, a method of evading the void.

For instance, I can play the bootleg of the Cat Power solo show from the Bumbershoot Festival at the Seattle Opera House on September 6, 1999—I treasure knowing the concert's exact date and location: the recording a relic of an otherwise irretrievable time and place— and one hour will elapse, in my anxiety of the present time and place, with an increased degree of peace: Chan Marshall's voice, the most soothing sound I've ever encountered.

*

Chan's pivotal album *The Greatest* marked its tenth anniversary the year I began writing this: at the end of 2016—a critical breaking point in the United States, when the incoming presidential adminis- tration brought into sharpest focus the most destabilizing elements of our society, catalyzing seismic shifts among personal, national, and global discourses, with aftershocks that reverberate to this day. At the end of 2016, I worried that the limited rights of queer and other marginalized Americans would become increasingly imperiled. Also at the end of 2016, my partner and I had been together for five of ultimately ten years. Anxiously attached, I worried over his fidelity and safety while neglecting my well-being; I worried over any possible threat to the relationship's longevity. Cat Power bootlegs provided reifying, life-affirming comfort, through the continuity of my repeated listening. And what I heard there, I was called to write here.

The Greatest, Chan's seventh LP, represents a crucial turning point in her career as Cat Power. Recorded during three days in May 2005 at Ardent Studios in Memphis, and released on January 20, 2006, the album was the outcome of collaborating with an ensemble—including legendary musicians such as Teenie Hodges—named the Memphis Rhythm Band.

Chan had composed songs for *The Greatest* on piano and guitar without transcribing chords. Upon meeting her new bandmates, she played the tunes solo, and they charted along using the Nashville number system—a method of noting chord progression with numbers instead of letters. In *Fader* magazine, she's quoted: "We would get into the studio and I would play a song. They'd listen to it and then Teenie would say, 'Now, Chan, was that 5-5-1-5 or 5-1-1-5?'... And then [they'd] go into the corner and work it out."

While these musicians played a major role in crafting the album tracks, the arrangements of the early solo renditions had been expanding—and, in performances on tour with the Memphis Rhythm Band and then with the Dirty Delta Blues, would continue to expand—like galaxies.

*

The performance is a place where Chan reaches extemporaneous precision of pitch and phrasing, surpassing the engineered finish of the multiple takes that produce the studio track. In person, in public, she excels at spontaneously conjuring the strife and triumph of the pain and joy that occasioned the song.

In a performance and, to an extent, on its bootleg, we the audience witness the artist incarnating their mythos—the ability and the behavior for which they're renowned. At the same time, the artist contradicts that mythos with their physicality, fallibility, mortality. Why can that be so enthralling? It's the allure of the occult of creativity: that rare, rhapsodic feeling we're witnessing—and, by extension, capable of—creation against constant deterioration.

*

At the end of 2016, as American politics imploded, I began orbiting around the Cat Power song "Could We." For ten years, I'd too-easily dismissed this entry on *The Greatest*—but when I heard its bootleg versions, my appreciation deepened, and the origins of this book emerged.

Likely Cat Power's most upbeat tune—honky-tonk horn section, sanguine bass line, sugary lyrics—it effuses the charm of a romantic comedy theme song. In fact, it was featured in a movie, *Boyhood*, playing on the car radio as the narcissistic father pulls over to scold his kids for being aloof, projecting his own aloofness onto the kids, as narcissistic fathers often do. I found this an odd pairing.

Through the lyrical arc of "Could We," an intricate narrative unfolds in minimal movement. Five sparse verses deftly convey the neuroses of a new relationship: first flirtation, first date, first kiss, first sleepover, and the proposal of a second date. The early bootlegs of the song possess a distinct melancholy (wistful, pining, lonely)—I listen and picture the singer nervously rocking in a rocking chair, on the front porch of a house at the dead end of a dirt road, crooning to take her mind off waiting for a crush to call—however, the later bootlegs provide vivid evidence of Chan's evolving self-discovery, as her demeanor brightens and her courage burgeons.

But for ten years, I skipped the studio track, turned off by its extroversion. Then, at the end of 2016, determined to learn some coping mechanisms for the anxiety of love and loss, I taught myself how to praise it.

*

"Could We" opens Chan's solo show at the Earl in her hometown, Atlanta, on May 4, 2004.

This is its earliest known recording: a timid invocation (*Could we? Take a walk? Could we? Have a talk alone*) to the most intimate audience—so intimate that, later in the set, someone repeatedly requests the song "Wealthy Man," and Chan responds: "Dinette, will you *please* hush?" Here, it's her homecoming crowd—people who must've attended the inaugural Cat Power shows a decade prior.

Now, playing the intro to "Could We," Chan strums back and forth between two chords, briskly, then stops and says: "I gotta slow down." (After singing, she'll explain: "I am *trippin'* on Red Bull.") The strumming resumes—more pensive, expansive, windy, shimmery: pale bronze sunlight on a dirt road in the middle of spring— and when she begins singing, the road turns into a pasture, rolling uninterrupted for acres and acres. Chan's timbre, at its most resonant, reaches a frequency that gives me the sensation of an opening: mind momentarily transcending body, merging with the abyss that is this universe.

April 28, 2005, at Queen Elizabeth Hall in London: This ninety-minute set starts with a harrowing rendition of the song "Hate." Chan warbles: *I hate myself*—she strums the guitar—*and I want to die.*

I've found roughly ninety seconds of video footage from this show, wherein Chan's hunched over the piano, her face hidden behind long bangs, her disposition laden with the freight of a mind that entraps and is trapped by its body—singing as though bereft of these songs, she'd dissipate. This performance is her sixteenth of the year and her seventh of the month (less than two weeks after the first time I saw her on stage: April 16, at Purchase College)—and she has toured essentially nonstop for a decade. Four days before this, she played in Stockholm. Two days hence, she'll play in Glasgow. The next month, she'll play eight dates in Australia. And the following month, she'll make a breakthrough album, *The Greatest*, in Memphis.

But here, inside an auditorium on London's Belvedere Road, she performs eleven of the twelve songs that will constitute *The Greatest* (including "Hate")—and they're delicately drawn, darkly shaded sketches of what they'll become.

Eighteen minutes into the concert, she strums the intro to "Could We," and the atmosphere evokes a cloudless sky, the repeating chords as steady as a stretch of desert highway, her voice a falcon soaring overhead. This moment is singularly uplifted in a predominantly brooding performance. But no matter how depleted Chan's energy may be, she gives everything left to these songs. With her whole consciousness concentrated on her breath, Chan transforms into "a column of air"—as Allen Ginsberg once observed of Bob Dylan—the inhale silent, so the exhale seems contiguous: a continuous tunnel of sound, pure sound.

Sixteen months later—August 25, 2006—in a solo show at Malibu Performing Arts Center, Chan's presence sounds emboldened after having toured for the past four months with the support of the Memphis Rhythm Band. As she plays "Hate," she sings: *I do not hate myself and I do not want to die.** Still, she's hypercritical of the sound—perhaps newly unaccustomed to the nudity of performing by herself. Concluding "Hate," she quibbles that the guitar is "crispy"—and, later, that the piano is "hot"—as she frequently pauses to ask the sound engineer for more reverb.

"I just love reverb on the vocal," she tells the audience. "I actually sing, or project, more when there's reverb. Because when there's not, I tend to reserve. But when there's like a lot of room, I tend to project more—and relax."

Despite that, the overall climate feels more clement here in Malibu than it did at Queen Elizabeth Hall. Halfway into the set, she strums the intro to "Could We" and it's so relaxed—like a summer weekend with no plans, when a crush calls to see if I'm free, and I am, so the crush comes to meet me.

Tonight, Chan sings at the higher reaches of her range, where, in Atlanta and London, she sang low. In her lower register, the notes reach out to cradle her voice; in her high register, her voice reaches out to clasp the notes. Tonight, the word *we* goes up the scale after the word *could* (hopeful), where, in Atlanta and London, *we* went down the scale (doubtful).

This is the moment in the set that I cherish most: Concluding an exceptionally powerful and excruciatingly vulnerable performance of Otis Redding's "Remember Me," as the audience bursts into

---

* After I wrote this, Chan recorded these lyrics under the title "Unhate" for the Cat Power LP of 2022, *Covers*.

applause, Chan says into the microphone, apologetically: "That sucked."

Now, the Cat Power mythos becomes endearingly embodied: self-effacing humility—despite a superhuman feat of supreme beauty—in pursuit of the transcendence of mind beyond body, or what I eventually discovered Chan would call *openness*.

*

That Malibu set rivals an almost identical set a month later—September 5, 2006—at Boston's Museum of Fine Arts. This recording was made from the second show of the night. Over the decades, Chan has done dozens of double-headers; one in particular unspooled into a single prolonged concert—a nearly four-hour bootleg—at the Grog Shop in Cleveland, on November 20, 2013.

Tonight, in Boston, Chan plays "Could We" much later than usual—three songs from the end—as an afterthought. "Did I play this one yet?" she asks, strumming the intro—a meadow in the mountainous forest of this performance. Tonight, she's even more meticulously critical than she'd been the previous month in Malibu.

Beginning this set with "House of the Rising Sun" and abruptly abandoning it for "Love & Communication," she keeps pausing to ask for more reverb. After ten minutes of false starts, she explains: "It's hard to sing when it's real tight like that—like when you're singing in the shower, you don't sing against the tile." She laments: "The last show sounded more open."

*

Fast forward—2013, in an interview with German television show *aspekte*, at the Traumzeit Festival in Duisburg, Chan recounts a memory from childhood. During gym class, she'd wait to be alone in the locker room, then she'd sing in the tiled showers, which had, she recalls, "the most amazing reverb." Her peers overheard and asked her to sing for them. "That was probably the first time I performed," she says.

Studying the Cat Power records chronologically, we can trace a trajectory: a pursuit of the original reverb that Chan accessed in youth—the pursuit of reverb's openness, the openness that precedes our existence and awaits us after—the sound, nothing but air.

Alone with my turntable on Christmas in 2016, I played all my Cat Power records in one sitting (sadly excluding Chan's second album, *Myra Lee*, since it hasn't been, and should be, pressed on vinyl), spinning around six hours straight. I'd hoped to access that same openness: the transcendence of mind beyond body, which is liberation from the anxiety of loss and death.

*

"Now that we've been playing live it's so much more open and there's so much more room for [the band] as individuals to move and shimmy in the songs," Chan says in an interview coinciding with a concert for *Austin City Limits*, on September 18, 2006.

Accompanied by twelve musicians—two backup singers, three string-players, a drummer, trumpeter, saxophonist, bassist, and keyboardist, with Doug Easley on pedal steel and Teenie Hodges on guitar—she's becoming a lead singer. Almost completely confident at the microphone stand, she dances spiritedly, albeit bashfully—vulnerable without the shield of an instrument.

Though rumored that more than two hours were filmed, only thirty minutes aired. The most open moment: a medley of "Cross Bones Style" and "Nude as the News" that culminates in an ecstatic climax—the instruments vamping as Susan Marshall repeats: *He's related to you, he's related to you*; while Queen Ann Hines chants:

Un-believable, un-believable, un-believable things things things things; and Chan hollers: *Hater, I have your diamonds*—those lines overlapping again and again.

"I never really thought I was a singer," she says in the accompanying interview, but this isn't the only group that she's fronted. In the 1990s—performing with Glen Thrasher and Mark Moore, then Tim Foljahn and Steve Shelley, then Mick Turner and Jim White—she'd stand to the side, her back to the audience, far from the microphone, without much greater emphasis on her voice than on the drums and guitars. The bootlegs from this era are engulfed in the instruments—psychedelic, Hendrix-style guitars and thumping drums—drowning out the voice: the voice not yet afloat, not yet the open ocean that it is now.

By the time of *Austin City Limits* with the Memphis Rhythm Band, Chan has realized that singing's her calling; she's experimenting with how to manipulate her body to maximize its expressive capacity, using exaggerated facial expressions to modulate and amplify her vocals—the sound propelled by eccentric gestures of her arms and hands—into the ether. "Could We" is the one song in this set that Chan plays with the band on guitar—strumming her Danelectro U1—her longtime tour guitar.

I watch and listen, attempting to achieve a similar self-realization—internalizing and reinterpreting the openness I hear and see. I write—my voice breaks open on these pages, my mind transcends my body—and I am free.

*

October 22, 2006: Chan plays another solo show at the Earl in Atlanta, two-and-a-half years after the first set illustrated in this essay. "Could We" is one of two songs for which I've found footage, with three different videos of it posted online.

If the bootleg of 2004 sounded like embarking into the open, the bootleg of 2006 sounds like returning from the odyssey. Now, at the end of the second recorded song, "Say," Dinette's distinctive voice requests the song "Wealthy Man" again, as in 2004. Here, at Chan's sixtieth performance of the year, she's undaunted. Buoyant, she sits—the Danelectro U1 on her knee—she strums, bouncing in the chair like she wants to go faster and faster; she sings, thick with Dylan-esque inflection, projecting as though the band's there behind her; she beams at the audience between verses. *Let's make another date real soon, in the afternoon*, she concludes, then jokes in an exaggerated Southern accent: "That's a song about doin' it in the afternoon."

This is the Danelectro U1's final concert; it'll be broken six days later. It's also the last solo show Chan will play until September 18, 2013.

*

October 28, 2006: Cat Power and the Memphis Rhythm Band take to the Snake Eyes Stage at the Vegoose festival in Las Vegas. This video footage is tinted hazy greenish gold, suffused with the temperature of an unseasonably mild afternoon. I've rewatched it so often, I can't listen to the isolated audio without imagining those hues.

"The Greatest" kicks off this set—and most (if not all) of this era's sets with the band. One facet that distinguishes each performance: whether Chan climbs up or tumbles down the scale on the second half of the word "parade" in the phrase *the later parade*. At Vegoose, she climbs up to where the oxygen thins. I prefer the tumble down— verdant valley—which she does most gracefully four months earlier, in her luminous *Later with Jools Holland* performance of June 20.

Fifteen minutes into the Vegoose set, a stagehand approaches her.

"I guess the guitar never came," she says.

"It came, but it's broken," the stagehand responds.

"What do you mean?"

"The guitar's broken."

"How?"

The answer's inaudible. Chan's taken aback.

"'Could We' without guitar?" asks pianist Rick Steff.

Pacing the stage, Chan turns to the crowd and groans: "My guitar's broken!"

The band launches into "Could We," and the singer doesn't know what to do with her fidgeting hands. After fumbling the lyrics of the final two verses, when the instruments hold the closing chord, she says into the mic: "I'm distracted."

Here, now, I memorialize the Danelectro U1—an otherwise irretrievable relic. I build it this monument. I bring it back into time and place.

*

Two months later—December 7, 2006—at the Trans Musicales festival in Rennes, France, Chan exudes so much openness and vitality, I'll put on the professionally recorded footage for motivation in moments of exhaustion from anxiety.

Now touring with the Dirty Delta Blues—Judah Bauer, Gregg Foreman, Erik Paparazzi, and Jim White—Chan has brought together charismatic instrumentalists who ascend to the highest psychic plane while making music. Here, they play their intro to "Could We"—the bass plucked like a cocky stride alongside the staccato snare drum—and Chan speaks smilingly into the microphone: "Sad and groovy. Sad and groovy."

They jam for a minute, adoringly, as though diligently priming a massive canvas for the brushstrokes of her voice. Judah plays some sly, sexy riffs on the guitar. Gregg dangles a lit cigarette between his lips, with an unlit cigarette behind his ear; he slaps a tambourine on his hip and claps it against his palm; he sits down at the organ and swipes at the keys. I think of the lyric from "Lived in Bars," which they'll perform in this set: *Who's gonna play drums, guitar, or organ with chorus*—and I don't think she imagined, when she wrote that line, she'd finally find a group of musicians who'd be this simpatico.

Three-quarters through "Could We," Chan walks away from the mic. The band keeps grooving. Erik sways to and fro, bobbing his head. Jim keeps time, a boyish joy in his eyes and a devilish smile. The camera zooms in on their faces, their fingers, the guitar strings, the hi-hat. Judah riffs some more, while Chan consults about something (the sound? A bit later she'll say: "I wish it was louder—this room is too big for us") in earnest with Gregg, who then counts them off, and Chan delivers the final verse.

If her tone has encompassed a meadow, a pasture, a dirt road, a highway, the open ocean, and the endless sky, then at Trans Musicales, her tone encompasses a bridge—a suspension bridge—steely, towering, spanning two shores: self-consciousness and self-confidence. I build a bridge in parallel. It brings me from the former shore to the latter. I'm nearly there.

*

At the Chanel Haute Couture spring show in Paris, on January 23, 2007, Cat Power and the Dirty Delta Blues play onstage behind an audience in stadium seating, facing a gymnastics mat emblazoned with the Chanel logo, where ethereal models parade in luxurious garments. Performing to the back of the audience, Chan and the band appear more flexible without the pressure of the spectators' scrutiny, while they sound more rigid in their cadence, to which the models stay in step.

I call this short set the Catwalking Blues:

1) "Naked If I Want To" (*Would you let me walk down your street?*)

2) "Could We" (*Could we? Take a walk?*)

3) "(I Can't Get No) Satisfaction" (*When I'm driving in my car*)

4) "Tracks of My Tears" (*When you see me walking down the street*)

At the finale, the band reprises their intro to "Could We" as Karl Lagerfeld walks onto the runway, takes a bow, and blows a kiss to Chan.

*

More than a year later—a year that Chan and the Dirty Delta Blues spent playing multiple shows each month across America and around the globe—on May 30, 2008, at the Primavera Sound festival in Barcelona, the set has changed to mostly tunes from *Jukebox*, the Cat Power LP released four months earlier.

Here, Chan appears to achieve total self-actualization. Singing with the microphone in hand, rather than on a mic stand, she navigates the stage, lunging and jumping, using her whole body to form the tone. Although she glances offstage sporadically, points to the mic, then points upward—a signal to the audio engineer, meaning "more reverb"—the vocals reverberate with utmost openness; her voice echoes beyond certain phrases.

In the latter half of the set, while the band plays their intro to "Could We," Gregg says: "Ladies and gentlemen, brothers and sisters, let me get one second of your time: the woman you came to see—"

"Me!" Chan bellows, unabashedly.

Asked by Spotify, in 2012, what were the five albums that shaped Chan's life, the singer says: "Five albums that made me who I am at forty? The first one would be a bootleg that I can't find by Otis Redding."

At age twelve, she'd found, in her father's music collection, a reddish-orange record-sleeve bearing the image of a man in a sharkskin suit. "The first song on that record is called 'These Arms of Mine,'" she remembers. "When you put the needle down, the first thing I heard was glass." Clinking a glass, she exclaims: *These arms of mine!*

The concert was supposedly in Paris, and for years, she has perused live recordings from Paris but hasn't tracked down this specific performance. "That's the one that electrocuted my brain," she says.

Here, now, I can say the same of "Could We" and its bootlegs.

*

On September 30, 2018, I attended a Cat Power show at Forest Hills Stadium in Queens, New York; by this point, I'd seen Chan on so many occasions, I'd lost count. A few days after the performance, a full-length bootlegged video surfaced online. About twenty seconds into the recording, I hear my voice: a *woo*, or a *who*—an articulation of uninhibited pleasure—a cheer, which you can hear between practically every song in the set. When I watch or listen to this bootleg, I cringe.

As you vocalize, both external ("air-conducted") and internal ("bone-conducted") sound is processed by your inner ear's cochlea, where, according to Timothy E. Hullar in an article for *Scientific American*, "the mechanical properties of your head enhance [the voice's] deeper, lower-frequency vibrations... When you listen to a recording of yourself speaking, the bone-conducted pathway that you consider part of your 'normal' voice is eliminated, and you hear only the air-conducted component in unfamiliar isolation." (Tellingly, many people dislike the air-conducted sound of their voice, preferring the deeper, lower—or more conventionally masculine—and "normal" bone-conducted sound.)

My voice in this bootleg is that uncanny—as unfamiliar and yet fundamental as my own blood.

Nevertheless, this footage remains paramount in my collection. Singing the set-opener ("He Turns Down"), Chan sees me in the audience, smiles, points, winks, and puts her right hand on her chest above her heart. When I listen without watching, I hear her smile in her voice.

*

"I sing to use the Waiting," wrote Emily Dickinson in a poem of 1864.

We live by waiting; we're creatures who've sung to survive. Will our songs outlast us?

Emily—already ready to go—always anticipated the arrival of some companion ("God"?) who'd be her guide.

In this way, Chan's voice has guided me, and it accompanies me still, in singing myself through the vacuous, interminable delay of the vexing, inescapable day-to-day.

I SING TO USE THE WAITING
On Stuck Song Syndrome

While a song plays on a loop in my mind, I'm free from the infinity of anxious, obsessive, self-hating, self-punishing thoughts that would otherwise spiral there. My waking hours become distinguished by one song or a few—the playlist depends on my mood or, maybe, determines my mood; every morning, immediately upon rousing from sleep, I hear, inwardly, a lyric that speaks to me, a melody that soothes me, and I bring it along through the day—marking time, marking time by its repetition. I recite it in silence on the subway. I hum or whistle it at work. I belt it out of tune when I get home.

But the condition of having a lyric or melody repeating in the mind to an excessive extent has been pathologized as *stuck song syndrome*. Neuroscientists call the song in question *involuntary musical imagery*, or an *earworm*, inspired by the German use of *ohrwurm* (an earwig) to name the phenomenon. Oliver Sacks called it a *brainworm*. Theodor Reik, Freud's protégé, called it *the haunting melody*.

Some involuntary musical imagery can disturb the hearer, and thus, I suppose, it deserves the uncomfortable connotations of worming: writhing, tunneling. If the haunting melody disturbs me, I switch to another, more pleasurable one—dubbed a *cure tune* by Victoria Williamson and her colleagues in their paper "Sticky Tunes: How

Do People React to Involuntary Musical Imagery?" Cure tunes linger, ghostlike, whispering down the passages of my memory. My primary stream of consciousness sounds like scanning the preset channels on a satellite radio—a medley of involuntary musical imagery—not an *ohrwurm* but an ouroboros: the snake with its tail in its mouth. I overhear a familiar lyric or melody, and it sticks instantly. Choosing a cure tune, I snag on a phrase that I turn into a refrain; I curate an anthology of refrains. Merely glimpsing a song's title lodges its refrains in the foreground of my focus. An event or statement triggers my recollection of a refrain, and I say it aloud in response. For a decade, I'd conjure the introductory piano chords of "Willie" from Cat Power's record *The Greatest* to neutralize intrusive thoughts. Now, every few weeks, a new song announces itself as the one I call *my anthem*—one that enables me to feel "alive and connected to the world," as a friend of mine described the effect—and I listen through earphones in three or four or a dozen takes per hour. Frequently, I get the urge to restart the song before it is finished—exemplary of my tendency to demand more and more of the things I already possess. My anthem, at the time of writing, mashes up several tracks from Ariana Grande's album *thank u, next*.

I must've been younger than twelve when I began using anthems to modulate anxiety. On March 9, 1998, the sitcom *Ally McBeal* aired the seventeenth episode of its first season, and I watched it on television. "You need a theme song," Ally's new therapist, Tracey, played by guest star Tracey Ullmann, tells her. "Something that you can play in your head to make you feel better." (Ironically, Ally does, in fact, have an extra-textual theme song: the show's opening credits, "Searchin' My Soul" by Vonda Shepard.)

"Do you have one?" Ally asks.

"Since I was ten," Tracey responds. "And it still works." Putting "Tracy" by the Cuff Links on the stereo, she says, "Every time I feel down, I hear it in my head."

"You sing *this* in your head?" Ally asks, incredulously, though later, she'll pick two of her own theme songs: "O-o-h Child," popularized by the Five Stairsteps, and "Tell Him," popularized by the Exciters. I remember watching, buoyed by the elation of self-identification, thinking, *I do that, too.*

However, I didn't hear about this habit in terms of pathology until I saw Jeremy O. Harris's *Slave Play* on Broadway in October 2019. Within the second act, it's revealed that the protagonists have come together in a form of group couples' therapy called Antebellum Sexual Performance Therapy—a fictional role-playing treatment that confronts the violence perpetuated by racism in the lives and inter-racial relationships of the patients—and they receive the diagnoses of "obsessive-compulsive disorder / with acute musical-obsessive disorder." The play's central character, Kaneisha, endures *musical hallucinations*—a severe form of stuck song syndrome, in which the hearer believes their involuntary musical imagery originates from an external source—and these diagnoses set the stage for her emotional breakthrough, delivered in an impassioned anti-colonial monologue that enunciates her trauma. Kaneisha's earworm, Rihanna's "Work," resounds overhead in moments of pleasure and distress, accentuating and superseding her revelatory orations.

If I remember correctly, the production I saw on this evening in October 2019 introduced the concept that involuntary musical imagery may elapse at half the song's actual speed in the mind of the hearer. And, if I remember correctly, following the performance, as the audience exited the John Golden Theatre in Manhattan, "Work" resounded overhead at half speed—an immersive imitation, reinforcing this concept. Soon after, I discovered a bootleg of my personal anthem at the time, Cat Power's "Woman"—a session from the BBC Radio 6 Music studio in London on October 22, 2018, when she performed a solo piano rendition at a markedly slower tempo, if not quite half, compared to the version on her record *Wanderer*.

Such synchronicities reassured me that the peculiarities of my haunting melodies weren't anomalous. And yet, in the edition of the *Slave Play* script published by Theatre Communications Group, no trace of this half-tempo concept remains, and the only reference to any alteration of the earworm resides in these lines from Gary, whose musical hallucinations feature Unknown Mortal Orchestra's "Multi-Love": "It didn't sound the way it normally does / it was like / it was amplified or something?"

A study conducted by James J. Kellaris in 2003 at the University of Cincinnati found that more than 98 percent of the population encounters earworms, although true *musical obsessions* are considered rather rare, occurring predominantly among people diagnosed with obsessive-compulsive disorder. Musical obsessions involve "persistent sounds or tunes, not controlled by the will, that cause clinically significant anxiety and distress," whereas stuck song syndrome "can be distressing" but "does not deteriorate the quality of life of the individual," according to Juan Manuel Orjuela Rojas and Ingrid Lizeth Lizarazo Rodríguez in their paper "The Stuck Song Syndrome: A Case of Musical Obsessions." At worst, my haunting melody disrupts my attention to conversation or contemplation—ever so slightly dissociating my imagination from reality. I am lucky to have randomly developed the methods dubbed *engagement* and *distraction* by Victoria Williamson and colleagues for coping with sticky tunes—and am ultimately transfigured, not trapped, by this experience.

Daniel J. Levitin's *This Is Your Brain on Music* devotes only one paragraph to involuntary musical imagery, declaring that earworms resemble auditory short-term memory: the recall of sonic information fifteen to thirty seconds in length. Further, Levitin suggests that haunting melodies illustrate how the brain creates memory, in that the hearer's neurons, during sonic recall, form a network identical to the network formed upon originally processing the information. "Our best explanation is that the neural circuits representing a song get stuck in 'playback mode,'" writes Levitin. But what precisely constitutes playback mode? The author doesn't elaborate.

Researchers believe they have pinpointed where—the rostromedial prefrontal cortex—and how the brain produces involuntary musical imagery, but the reasons why remain inconclusive. Wondering what's so irresistible about certain songs, Oliver Sacks's *Musicophilia* asks, "Is it some oddity of sound, of timbre or rhythm or melody? Is it repetition? Or is it arousal of special emotional resonances or associations?" Without providing a definitive verdict, Sacks offers a persuasive case for all the above. It's true, timbre, rhythm, and melody communicate more psychological nuance than language alone—rendering legible the most incomprehensible emotions—enunciating distress and amplifying pleasure. If a particular timbre, rhythm, or melody corresponds with a particular memory of profound emotion, then perhaps the activation of this emotional memory activates the recall of this sonic information—and vice versa.

Theodor Reik's *The Haunting Melody* also underscores the significance of analyzing the emotional resonance in musical associations: "The recurring tune may announce in its compelling and compulsive pressure the working of an unknown power in you. Whatever secret message it carries, the incidental music accompanying our conscious thinking is never accidental." Reik intimates that the subconscious articulates using involuntary musical imagery, and I do believe that a haunting melody has something to tell the hearer: something they need to know, something they already know but haven't fully fathomed.

Quite often, a lyric or melody from my past resurfaces, causing a tsunami of nostalgia (traversing the Manhattan Bridge on bike, I'll hear "Sirens" by Hop Along, Queen Ansleis—transporting me to senior year of undergrad, when I finally learned how to cycle). Yes, it tells me, you're feeling that old feeling again; you've always been this impatient, insecure creature; this song was then and still is here now

to help to heal you; it's not too late to learn patience and self-suffi-
ciency. And so, I say, "I sing to use the Waiting"—the first line of
that poem of 1864 by Emily Dickinson. The speaker of the poem
and I stand by the front door, ready to go, anticipating the arrival of
someone with whom we'll "journey to the Day / and tell each other
how We sung / to Keep the Dark away."

A lot of life is waiting. Using the waiting, the one who waits doesn't
wait in vain. I think I worry to use my waiting, and to use my worry, I
keep writing these words. Stuck songs and cure tunes accompany me
through spells of anxiety, boredom, loneliness—for I am terrified of
loneliness and prefer intimacy with friends and lovers over the sadness of solitude (expecting a phone call or text message, I'll listen to
Blondie's cover of "Hanging on the Telephone" by the Nerves—or
Cat Power's lustrous cover of it, a fragment of forty-two seconds
recorded for a Cingular Wireless commercial). Even the most banal
jingle, even the most disruptive ditty provides a minuscule degree of
amusement and continuity in place of anxiety and boredom. And
when solitude feels too terrible, while I'm anticipating the next intimacy—if I'm so lonely, I'm scared the sadness won't ever subside—
I play a song. It reminds me who I am—and how I want to be.

TOO GOOD TO WORK

On Rihanna

1. WORK

Rihanna had planned to take a year off.

In November 2013, following the Diamonds World Tour—ninety-six concerts in eight months on five continents—she intended not to return to the recording studio. Up to that point, she'd released one new album annually for seven years. "I wanted to have a year to just do whatever I want, artistically, creatively," she said in *Vogue*'s cover story of April 2016. "I lasted a week."

From March to June of 2018, I desperately looked for work. I'd been fired from my psychologically taxing job of seven years—a position that I should've quit after a week. But during those three months of unemployment, when I'd exhausted the day's job postings, I had time to do whatever I wanted. And so, while listening to Rihanna obsessively, I started writing again.

*

Instead of taking the intended hiatus, Rihanna began recording her eighth album, *Anti*—released in January 2016—her first LP with

Westbury Road Entertainment, the label she'd founded in 2005, named for the street where she was raised in Bridgetown, the capital of Barbados.

"FourFiveSeconds" was the first single of Rihanna's singing to be released through Westbury Road, in January 2015—featuring Kanye West and Paul McCartney—a freestanding track, unattached to an album. Here, her narrator proclaims that she's overworked; according to the lyrics, it's Tuesday, and she's irritable—already ready for the weekend—away from home, anxious to return on Monday the next week. Here, her elocution sounds rather anglicized in comparison to the Barbadian intonations of her speaking voice—those throaty, oblong vowels and quick, toothy consonants—her street-smart, world-wise timbre, which became distinctive immediately upon the premiere of "Pon de Replay" from her debut LP, *Music of the Sun*, in 2005. That year, a reporter for MTV News asked her: "When you're an older lady—and you're about to retire—what is the thing you want to be remembered for?"

"Remembered as Rihanna," she responded. "Remembered as being the artist from the Caribbean who came here and made it. And made it internationally."

While Barbados remains her unequivocal home base, indeed, she dwells in multiplicity—of music genres and national identities—of vocabularies and pronunciations. Multiplicity is Rihanna's forte; her inimitable sound, her indomitable style, and her tenacity—her good, hard work—all highlight the intersections and harmonize the parallels between personal and global histories.

*

The history of contemporary Barbadian music could be said to have started with resistance to its repression.

Beginning in the late 1620s and up to the mid-1830s, hundreds of thousands of people from Africa were enslaved by English colonists on sugarcane plantations that overtook Barbados. The colonists, who enforced the use of the English language and forbade the use of tribal languages, also instituted laws around 1660 that prohibited African musical expression, banning drums and horns, which could be used to communicate in code.

Resilient and resourceful, the African people enslaved in Barbados fashioned instruments from available materials, and the tuk band emerged—an ensemble of snare and bass drums, rattle, banjo or fiddle, and later, triangle and tin whistle—essentially obtaining the colonists' approval by imitating the colonial military bands. Curwen Best writes, in *The Popular Music and Entertainment Culture of Barbados*: "It is during the early and ensuing decades on the plantation, when the expressive culture of the slaves came into contact with formal cultural institutions such as the British marching band, that tuk aesthetics began to fully take shape, as African Barbadians absorbed other forms for the sake of their own survival... Tuk culture is therefore defined in its early manifestation as having to do with survival, adaptation, and dynamic negotiation." This tenacity—this good, hard work—is the recurring theme of music history in the Caribbean. Resisting repression, the African Barbadians sustained a musical tradition—despite life-threatening, world-destabilizing circumstances—by creating new modes of expression in forms of art that continue to evolve to this day.

*

In January 2016, Rihanna released the first single from *Anti*, featuring her longtime collaborator, Drake: "Work"—its lyrics mixing American English and Caribbean vocabulary and syntax, its instrumentation and rhythm inspired by the genre called dancehall.

Dancehall dates to 1970s Kingston, Jamaica, and developed out of the 1850s Jamaican dancehall scene formed by the Black population in reaction to exclusion from the white population's segregated indoor dances. The earliest dance halls took place in makeshift outdoor venues—back alleys, front yards—where "jive, jitterbugging, 'jogging,' arm-swinging, rolling, hip-wagging, shaking and waltzing were typical for the rumbas, waltzes and mento played by live bands using guitars and violins," writes Sonjah Stanley Niaah, in *DanceHall: From Slave Ship to Ghetto.* "Whether on ship decks, in school rooms or shrubs, or on the streets, the enslaved and, later, the freed Africans or peasantry settling across the island of Jamaica, and especially in Kingston, occupied marginal lanes... not only for housing and subsistence, but for performance as well. Articulation of the self in these spaces was, and continues to be, potent, as their marginalization is at once their power." With Jamaican dancehall, as with the Barbadian tuk band (two centuries and twelve hundred miles away), an expressive possibility flourished out of an impossibility, a prohibition; what started in provisional spaces moved and morphed, from the 1850s to 1970s, into a specific sound (drum cadences and synthesizer chords) and style (dance moves and club scenes), which resonate through "Work" from its opening instrumentals to its closing vocals.

"The recoding of the mainstream perception of the margin, in deploying its potential to create and communicate a sense of identity, is indicative of power," writes Niaah. "Creations such as Jamaican dancehall that achieve global recognition emerge in only a few centres on Earth, with power enough to interpolate, even disturb, state consciousness." Therefore, the dancehall performer not only enacts the resilience and resourcefulness of African culture within Caribbean history but also, by recoding the mainstream perception of the margin, performs an act of queerness. And therefore, Rihanna should be celebrated for her queer powers of survival, adaptation, and dynamic negotiation in her articulation of selfhood; by recoding the mainstream perception of the margin, she has flourished at the forefront of a history of racist and sexist material conditions and has achieved international, astronomical popularity.

*

When "Work" debuted, Rihanna's queer pronunciation of the track's multilingual lyrics confounded some listeners, who hastily disparaged the song in the vein of *The New York Times* critic Jon Caramanica's Eurocentric sentiments: "A pop-dancehall number that's all bubble and no depth, it's cheaply effective. In places, she barely even relies on words, truncating her syllables past patois to something far less exact." Now, the narrator of "Work" says the word *work* seventy-eight times. The narrator says more than four hundred words total, in American English and Caribbean vocabulary and syntax, and while not all phrases may be instantaneously legible to a Eurocentric listener, the sentiments aren't difficult to decipher.

One plausible reading of the narrative in "Work": The narrator is *at* work (and has been there probably every day this week), alternately addressing two parties—a confidant and a lover. Perhaps the narrator is so busy, stressed, and tired that she *can't* rely on words and *must* truncate her syllables in order to communicate efficiently. Perhaps the lover is at work as well; the narrator sends multiple missives, to no response. Rebuffed, the narrator reconsiders the romantic effort, venting frustration to both the confidant and the lover.

And then, Drake's voice chimes in:

> *Yeah, OK*
> *You need to get done, done, done at work*
> *Come over...*

It doesn't matter what's said next. The lover has received the message and has reciprocated—saying come over, saying everything's OK.

2. TOO GOOD

"Work" wasn't the only exchange of assurances between these lovers through narration by Rihanna and Drake. The singers had collaborated twice before, and they'd collaborate once more after "Work"—culminating in four tracks loosely connected by one narrative arc, which I traced again and again during my three months of unemployment, while also desperately looking for work. I'd send out a batch of applications, then trudge to Prospect Park, where I'd sit and smoke spliffs, listening to a playlist of these four tracks on a loop in my earphones.

The quartet commences in 2010 with "What's My Name?"—Rihanna's eighth number-one single on the *Billboard* Hot 100 (and her third that year)—the second single released from *Loud*, her fifth LP. "The track draws upon the warm island pop of her earlier material by lacing a heavy reggae beat with synthesized organs," reads the *Billboard* review. "As much as 'What's My Name' is a joint effort, Rihanna owns the song by delivering a more polished version of her pop persona." Now, the Eurocentric conception of a polished persona is what "Work" would be ignorantly measured against (does *polished* mean *anglicized?*)—and to call this island pop or reggae seems vague, inaccurate, even ahistorical. Could the cadence of the snare drum compare to that of the tuk band instead? Maybe not: The track's songwriting and production teams are best known for their work in R&B and hip-hop. But it's true, Rihanna not only excels vocally and dominates lyrically, she also takes control of the narrative that initiates the romance between her and Drake's personae.

Here, her effervescent voice opens the tune: *Oh na-na*, she sings (already playing with syllables) and then chants the song's title. Drake takes the opening verse—his voice: somewhat adolescent (he was twenty-three at the time), not exceptionally pleasing (nasally, congested), albeit undeniably charismatic—his sheer presence more compelling than his message and delivery. When Rihanna takes the chorus, she propels the quartet's central premise on course: She's *looking for a guy to put in work*. This narrative portrays these lovers delaying parting after their first sleepover, flush with the roseate tones of waking beside a new crush; Rihanna's hairstyle resembles such a pinkish red on the *Loud* album cover and in its accompanying visuals—including the "What's My Name?" music video, wherein the two singers simulate the events that led to the lyrics' scenario: They meet in a bodega in Manhattan's Lower East Side, they go to her place and drink some white wine; she washes the wine glasses, he makes a move. They caress, embrace, kiss, and the narration finds them the next morning. They're smitten. He flirts, tempting her to stay. She has to leave for work.

*

"Take Care"—Rihanna and Drake's second collaboration—was the fifth single from Drake's second LP, 2012's *Take Care*. Here, his voice is bright and warm—much more mature than two years prior—but it doesn't hold a candle to Rihanna's radiant tone. She opens with a phrase from "I'll Take Care of You," written by Brook Benton and recorded by Bobby Bland in 1959. In 2010, Gil Scott-Heron covered the song on his final LP, *I'm New Here*, then in 2011, Jamie xx remixed Scott-Heron's rendition and retitled it "I'll Take Care of U," which Jamie xx thoroughly sampled when he produced Drake and Rihanna's "Take Care."

The music video—centered on airbrushed footage of the singers caressing and embracing—omits Rihanna's introductory refrain, opening instead with an original verse by Drake. Now, his persona mirrors his gestures in their previous pas de deux—his charismatic flirtation, his penchant for partying (*I'll get high if I want to*, he brags, reminiscent of his *good weed, white wine* in "What's My Name?")—though he admits to hearing rumors about the reputation of Rihanna's persona in her past affairs. And yet, it hasn't changed his mind; he admits to having a similarly salacious reputation, and he's ready to forfeit the nightlife for the comforts of home. Closing the song, Rihanna reiterates the refrain. She hasn't changed her mind, either. She's ready to take care of him.

During my unemployment, when my partner would leave for work, I'd lie on the bed, looping this four-track playlist in my earphones, worried over taking care of my partner—and barely taking care of myself—but consoled and bolstered by these songs.

*

In February 2016, "Work" was released with two different music videos.

One video's set inside Toronto's The Real Jerk restaurant, where a dancehall party takes place: Rihanna and Drake—at opposite sides of the space—bounce among friends, drinking Red Stripe and smoking spliffs. Moving across the crowd, they approach each other; they meet, they caress and embrace; she grinds on him, she twerks.

The other video finds Rihanna and Drake alone together in a non-descript living room, bathed in hot pink and cool blue neon light; she lip-synchs three-quarters of the song in the foreground—he watches, riveted, from a sofa in the background—until they trade spots for his verse. Caressing and embracing through the final verse, they grind. She twerks.

"While mainstream critics may be uncomfortable with Rihanna's gyrations or misconstrue her patois as gibberish, ['Work'] is an example of an unapologetic black woman proudly showing her heritage," wrote Taj Rani, in *Billboard*, where it topped the Hot 100 chart. Likewise, Rihanna's decision to return from a four-year lapse following a seven-year streak in releasing LPs, a lapse during which she unflaggingly *worked*, by releasing "Work"—risking the ridicule of Eurocentric listeners accustomed to her anglicized elocution—furthermore, Rihanna's entire courageous career thus far enacts a singularly liberating experience of identity expression.

*

"Too Good"—Rihanna and Drake's fourth and last collaboration to date—was the fifth single from Drake's fourth LP, 2016's *Views*, released seven months after "Work."

This track remains an outlier in the quartet: the only one without a music video and the only one not to reach the top ten of the Hot 100 (peaking at number fourteen). However, *Billboard* ranked it number thirty-two of their 100 Best Pop Songs of 2016, citing: "The addition of Caribbean queen Rihanna on this dueling duet takes [Drake's] island vibe to the next level. Don't be fooled by the *Views* track's sunny beat, though: These two should really break up, if they know what's good for them." Now, the lovers reach an impasse, unable to efficiently communicate. Drake takes the opening verse, announcing that he no longer knows how to talk to her. Here, again, his persona reflects some earlier gestures (*I got high as the expectations*, he boasts)—his voice at its most appealing (smoother, richer)—but he's no longer the charmer he was in the preceding narratives; he realizes he's *too good* for the relationship. Rihanna rejoins, her voice lush and lucid: She no longer knows how to talk to him, either—she has to *work too hard* for him—she also *got high as the expectations*; she realizes she's *too good* for the relationship, too. Equally self-possessed and assertive, she disqualifies his claim to superiority. *I'm too good for you*, they serenade each other in unison.

The lovers surrender, in the end—or until the singers' next collaboration.

BALLAD OF ROBYN AND WHITNEY

On Whitney Houston

PRELUDE

When I was eight weeks old, my mother had to go back to work.

In a letter to one of my aunts, dated November 1986, my mother wrote: "We have a sitter—a woman less than a mile from the house—I just hope she can handle him. He's a demanding kid—into people and body contact—he's not too crazy about entertaining himself."

My first babysitter would leave me alone after I'd fallen asleep—she'd hang out at the general store (one of the employees told my parents so)—and, in what I consider my earliest memory, I retain the faintest impression of two adult bodies hovering while a woman's voice attempts to console me; somehow, I'd understood that she'd been away, maybe because I'd been awake before she'd returned.

My second babysitter considered my desire for coddling to be too high-maintenance—according to my mother, who found me, on my last day in said babysitter's care, in the backyard, shrieking, strapped in a bassinet facing direct sunlight.

At twelve months, I entered daycare, where I went daily, for nine hours a day, until age five. There, I first apprehended the hollowness of hours—and there, I remember gradually comprehending the lapsing of time—around 2:00 in the afternoon (even now, I can recall the white plastic, black-numbered clock on the wall), I'd start to sob, inconsolable, uncertain how to sublimate my solitude, terrified that my mother wouldn't return.

PART ONE

1.

Before Robyn Crawford published a memoir in 2019, she last publicly acknowledged her integral role in Whitney Houston's life by writing an elegy for *Esquire* magazine the day after Whitney passed away, in 2012. Recounting their chance encounter during the summer of 1980, when Whitney was sixteen and they both worked at a community center in New Jersey, Robyn writes, "She introduced herself as 'Whitney Elizabeth Houston,' and I knew right away she was special."

Robyn went on to revolve around the innermost circle of Whitney's vast orbit—until their fateful estrangement in 2000. Through two decades, they faced persistent pressure to define and defend the parameters of their intimacy; their connection was ruthlessly scrutinized by the entertainment media, music industry, audience, church, and family.

Robyn's memoir, *A Song for You*, depicts their mutually compassionate companionship with clear-eyed hindsight on the writer's shifting position in the singer's precarious circuit of attachments. Beginning at a formative age, Robyn's identity developed simultaneously with Whitney's skyrocketing stardom—in the memoir, the writer refers to the launch of the singer's career as "my and Whitney's dream"—and they navigated the same pitfalls of professional, religious, and familial homophobia, as they struggled to maintain a bond at once romantic, paternal, and spiritual.

In the elegy, Robyn writes, "She looked like an angel. When my mother first met her, she laughed and said, 'You look like an angel, but I know you're not.' And she wasn't. But she looked like one."

2.

Two documentary films released within one year—*Whitney: Can I Be Me* (2017) and *Whitney* (2018)—both portray a family ensnared in a crisis of faith.

Whitney opens with a voice-over of the singer describing a recurring dream of outrunning a mysterious giant; she confides, "My mother always says, 'Well, you know, that's nothing but the devil, he's just trying to get you.'" After pausing, she adds, "There's been several times the devil has tried to get me, but he never gets me."

Born in 1963 and raised in a profoundly devout household, Whitney was the youngest child of Cissy Houston, who'd started singing at age five in a gospel group, the Drinkard Singers, with her siblings. From 1963 to 1969, Cissy recorded as part of the Sweet Inspirations (alongside her nieces, Dionne and Dee Dee Warwick), who were managed by Whitney's father's company, John Houston Entertainment. (John—who called Whitney "Nippy"—would eventually manage Whitney via her own company, Nippy, Inc.) In 1970, after having recorded several albums under different monikers, Cissy debuted the solo LP, *Presenting Cissy Houston*. And while the Houston parents traveled to promote Cissy's career, Whitney and her brothers would stay at the homes of friends and family members.

"She worked her ass off and spent time away from us in order to make things better," says Whitney's brother Gary, regarding Cissy, in

Whitney. "I remember me and my sister crying, sitting on the curb, every time my mother would pull off to go."

This traumatic scene of separation created the unstable conditions for Whitney's precarious circuit of attachments—and set the stage for the discord of her psychological demons—all facilitated, from the beginning, by the family business.

At age eleven, Whitney started singing with the New Hope Baptist Church of East Orange, New Jersey—where Cissy has been the choir director for more than fifty years—and by thirteen, Whitney was aspiring to become a professional performer. One night, before a show at the Manhattan club Mikell's, Cissy feigned illness so that Whitney, then sixteen or seventeen, would go onstage instead. There, imitating her mother's mannerisms, Whitney entered showbiz; returning to Mikell's for regular gigs, she was scouted by Clive Davis, who'd sign Whitney's first recording contract at eighteen.

"I taught Whitney," says Cissy, in *Can I Be Me*. "I taught her what she knew. She sang from her heart. She knew how. She learned how."

Likewise, Whitney learned from her parents their belief system, which delineated the limits of her identity. In *Can I Be Me*'s archival footage, Whitney says, "When you're raised in church, and you're raised in the background of god-fearing religion, it's instilled in you. There's a certain boundary that you don't cross. I could've gotten into a lot more trouble than I got into if I hadn't thought about, *oh, my mother's gonna kill me*, or, *oh, my father and mother's gonna be so disappointed*, or, *I know God's watching me*."

3.

"For a small child [the] parents are at first the only authority and the source of all belief," Sigmund Freud proposes in the essay "Family Romances." "The child's most intense and most momentous wish during these early years is to be like [the] parents…"

What Freud calls family romance commences when a child becomes disillusioned with their parents or guardians and begins desiring idealized, improved substitutes. Freud operates under some classist assumptions—his overarching theory: children embroiled in family romance would ultimately prefer guardianship of wealthier economic status—and from a heterosexist perspective (his underlying conclusion: children naturally identify with the guardian of their same gender). However, the kernel of truth in "Family Romances" proves fruitful in unearthing the roots of a crisis of faith. If the infant who idolizes their guardian is prone to inherit the guardian's belief system, then, as a child discerns that its guardians can be fallible—and that their belief systems can be faulty—the child must seek other idols. Often, one finds reverence for a religious authority—a god—an attentive and benevolent (albeit judging and sometimes punishing) father figure. Often, one finds loyalty to a lover—a partner—somebody to mother and be mothered by.

4.

"I had wanted to know the Word for myself, so when I was fifteen years old I read from Genesis straight through to Revelation," Robyn writes in *A Song for You*. "Whitney knew the Bible like the back of her hand."

Religious faith anchored Robyn and Whitney in the turbulent wake of their family romances. In a chapter of *A Song for You* titled "Separation Anxiety," Robyn describes Whitney's adolescence: "Her life was organized around going to church, choir rehearsals, and her mother's recording sessions." And yet, "Whitney couldn't talk to her mother—not about school and not about her feelings." Whitney needed a supplemental mother figure who could validate her individuality. This chapter also tellingly contains Robyn's memory from age twelve, when, immediately upon arrival at summer camp, she phoned her mother and asked to return home. "I was too worried to stay. I didn't know what would happen to Mom in my absence.

After that, Mom was concerned that I was too attached to her." Robyn needed a supplemental mother figure who could receive and reciprocate the intensity of her attachment style.

In the beginning, they sought stability in faith and found transcendence. Robyn pointedly remembers the first occasion when she'd witnessed Whitney singing: at New Hope Baptist Church, where the congregants ran ecstatically among the aisles, speaking in tongues, under the influence of Whitney's voice. "On that day, I sat in that church and I watched that little body stand there in that white robe and fill the place with her voice... in that moment, I realized that Whitney Elizabeth Houston *was* something else, something special—there was greatness and power pent up inside that body."

Then, they sought the transcendence of sex and intoxication. Robyn confides that by the time she and Whitney became physically intimate, they'd been using marijuana and cocaine habitually—disclosing that, while high, they'd "talk music and scripture for hours." Beneath their enduring faith, burgeoning addiction, and evolving attachment, an abysmal apprehension loomed. Robyn poignantly writes: "I continued to read the Bible on my own. I knew there had to be something more than what life had presented so far and it bothered me that the creation of human life was so amazing and yet finite. We are supposed to enjoy this journey but not hold on too tight to anyone or anything because, inevitably, it all goes away."

5.

John Bowlby's *Attachment and Loss*—the three-volume, foundational text on attachment theory, which posits that the dynamics of an infant's relationship with its primary guardian, specifically the mother figure, vitally influences the dynamics of all future relationships—studies how an infant's involuntary displacement from the mother figure may produce an effect that resembles Freudian trauma. Bowlby writes, "The psychological changes that regularly succeed the prolonged distress of separation are none other than repression, splitting, and denial... precisely the defensive processes that Freud postulates are the result of trauma." Additionally, Bowlby observed that an infant's involuntary displacement from a mother figure provoked a series of three reactions: protest, despair, and detachment.

> At first [the child] *protests* vigorously and tries by all the means available to [them] to recover [the] mother. Later [the child] seems to *despair* of recovering her but none the less remains preoccupied with her and vigilant for her return. Later still [the child] seems to lose [their] interest in [the] mother and to become emotionally *detached* from her... Thus the phase of *protest* is found to raise the problem of separation anxiety; *despair* that of grief and mourning; *detachment* that of defense.

If an infant's attachment to mother figure does vitally influence all future attachments, then the individual's future defenses—against the grief and mourning of involuntary displacement—may manifest in separation anxieties around other family members as well as friends and lovers, creating the unstable conditions for a precarious circuit of attachments. And, if an infant's primary scene of separation was exceptionally traumatic, then the individual may acquire an attachment style that repeats (to repair) the ensuing anxiety.

6.

The singer's chart-topping debut LP, 1985's *Whitney Houston*, was followed by the chart-topping *Whitney* in 1987, and by 1990—with the release of *I'm Your Baby Tonight*—she had become the employer of several family members and friends, including Robyn: as personal assistant and eventually as creative director. John Houston assumed the management position of Nippy, Inc.—putting "everybody in the family except Cissy" on the payroll, according to Steve Gittelman, the son of Whitney's first manager, who calls John "an opportunist" in *Whitney*. Both documentaries suggest that she unwittingly subsidized the incomes of numerous additional friends and family members. The turbulent wake of family romance continued to roil through the widening family business.

Also by this time, Robyn and Whitney had been living together for nearly a decade in an apartment in New Jersey. "Rumors had already started about her sexuality," says publicist Kenneth Reynolds in *Can I Be Me*. "Depending on who you were, you had to get through Robyn to get to Whitney. You have to understand the makeup of these guys who did promotion: seven hundred music program directors that are 99.9 percent heterosexual, 99.9999999 percent homophobic. And the rumor goes out that this woman is not a heterosexual. They had a field day with that."

Such speculation about Robyn and Whitney reduced their attachment to a tabloid spectacle, typecasting Robyn as the exemplar of queer seducer. Whitney's brother Michael calls Robyn by that same epithet—"an opportunist"—in *Whitney*. "She was something that I didn't want my sister to be involved with. It was evil. It was wicked," he says.

The family's faith in a religion that demonizes homoerotic desire—and their desire to participate in an economy that worships heterosexist, patriarchal ideals—prohibited an unconventional authority figure from fitting in Whitney's public image and private life.

In July 1992, Whitney married Bobby Brown: a high-profile union that allowed her to fill the frame of a normative American family.

7.

In *Ties That Bind*—a trailblazing exploration of familial homophobia, which transpires when a family unit excludes or diminishes the presence of its queer family members—Sarah Schulman ventures that a majority of queer individuals experience a phenomenon in common: "We have each, at some time in our lives, been treated shoddily by our families simply, but specifically, because of our homosexuality. This experience is, in turn, mirrored by the legal system and the dominant social structure within which gay people must live, as well as in the arts and entertainment industries, which select and control our representations."

While exceptions to this phenomenon gradually flourish, homophobia remains invasive and insidious within the majority of social units—from the home to the church and state. Thus, Shulman depicts the homophobic family member:

> They are being controlled by a broad, yet invisible, social force. Their own need for approval and the material privileges that approval accompanies, supersedes their love and acceptance of their family members and their sense of justice... It implies that the great social punishment that awaits detractors is so menacing that they will do anything to avoid it.

So many queer kids feel anomalous in their nuclear family, their extended family, their ancestry. So many have been made to feel like a broken link in their lineage.

To rectify this injustice, Schulman encourages "a reversed value in which it is the homophobe who is destroying the family, not the homosexual."

8.

Following Whitney's marriage to Bobby Brown, Robyn's narrative in *A Song for You* retains a noticeable distance from the singer's private life, and their paths approach a harrowing crossroads. But their trajectory had been obstructed by homophobia long before. A decade earlier, Robyn recalls:

> Whitney came by my mother's apartment and said she had a gift for me. She placed a box in my hands, and inside there lay a slate-blue Bible. She said that we shouldn't be physical anymore, because it would make our journey even more difficult. She also said she wanted to have children one day, and living that kind of life meant that we would go to hell.

Fear of religious persecution prevented Robyn and Whitney from further engaging in sexual intimacy; still, their attachment deepened its complexity. Shortly after that incident, they moved to their apartment in New Jersey—and later, to a mansion, where they lived with an assistant named Silvia, who provided a kind of parental supervision for the singer. At the onset of Whitney's celebrity, Robyn recalls:

> Whitney said, "I wish I could be two places at once, but I can't. I can handle the inside. I got this. But I need you on the outside looking in." I understood what I needed to do. If she didn't want you there, you weren't getting in, at least not through me. I was ready for this role, being out front when needed, getting things done, asking questions, or doing whatever was necessary to make things better and easier for Whitney.

Robyn readily accepted this position of guardianship in Whitney's circuit of attachments, but those homophobic obstacles proliferated; Robyn writes, "Her mother didn't like it at all and told Whitney, 'It's not natural for two women to be that close.'" Similarly, Whitney's father suggested the two feign dates with fake boyfriends in front of paparazzi.

And then, in 1990, a profile in *Fame* magazine portrayed the friends as lovers. Robyn writes: "That story altered the professional landscape for Whitney and me... Cissy insisted that I no longer walk next to Whitney in public. I couldn't ride in the car with her or sit next to her at most award shows."

When Bobby Brown entered the picture, Whitney's public image not only started to satisfy the heterosexist requirements of pop culture, it also began to undergo a hyperrealistic phase in her career. The original soundtracks for the films *The Bodyguard*, *Waiting to Exhale*, and *The Preacher's Wife*—released in 1992, 1995, and 1996, respectively—chronologically follow Whitney's first three studio LPs in her discography (she wouldn't release her fourth studio LP until 1998), and in each of these three films, Whitney plays the starring role. Each role epitomizes the fantasy of Whitney's private life at the corresponding point in her professional life; however, while performing the most normative iterations of her identity, her actual well-being declined in steep contrast to the thriving she enacted in character.

PART TWO

9.

Whitney's acting debut, *The Bodyguard*, premiered in November 1992, when she was twenty-nine.

The singer plays Rachel Marron, a singer who's expected to receive a nomination for a Best Actress award, with her recording of the film-within-the-film's theme song—"I Have Nothing"—topping the charts. Rachel is a single mother; her sister, Nicki, is employed as her personal assistant. Rachel's managers hire a new bodyguard, Frank, because a stalker has repeatedly attempted to murder her. Rachel objects to Frank's arrival—she's protective of her son, Fletcher, and vigilant not to disturb their household—but so far, the managers have kept her unaware of the stalker's threats.

In this universe of *The Bodyguard*, where Whitney Houston doesn't exist—and where Rachel Marron is the most successful singer-turned-actress in the world—the artist's Blackness is virtually immaterial, and racial inequities aren't addressed in the plot, so the violence of racism goes completely unacknowledged in this unreality of the silver screen. And still, heterosexist patriarchy inflicts damage under the guise of white men. The narrative valorizes the savior, Frank, as it villainizes the stalker, a middle-aged male with ghostly pale face and shoulder-length white hair, and it culminates in a spectacle of hetero-patriarchy: the gunman who shoots at Rachel—onstage, as she accepts the award—isn't the stalker; he's one of Frank's former colleagues, Portman, a charismatic British bodyguard whom Rachel seduces earlier in the film to make Frank jealous. Portman doesn't have an alibi, and his intentions aren't explained. A generalized, randomized, and eroticized threat ends up being most hazardous. This climax essentially re-creates Whitney's humiliation onstage at the Soul Train Awards in 1988, where she was jeered by the audience (and where she met Bobby Brown), but the redress doesn't entirely reclaim that traumatic event. Frank takes the bullet here, and Rachel cradles his body as he bleeds on her chest. Rachel nurses the hetero-patriarchal white savior back to life.

Rewind. See how the central themes of Whitney's trauma pervade the plot.

Rachel finally learns about the stalker, and she stops *protesting* Frank's presence. As he proves dependable, she warms to him; she even falls in love, according to the soundtrack's record-setting single, "I Will Always Love You."

But he refuses her affection. She *despairs*.

Then, she meets Portman at a party and seduces him, in Frank's presence. Avenging her frustration with Frank's refusal, she becomes uncooperative—*detached*—until the stalker threatens again, and she reattaches.

They hide out at Frank's father's woodland cabin, with Fletcher and Nicki. There, Nicki drunkenly divulges to Frank that she'd hired a hitman—claiming she was "very stoned" when she met the anonymous middleman, and admitting she was inspired by the stalker's death-threat letters, which expressed her own thoughts: "I hate her," she confesses. Now, the hitman breaks into the house, accidentally shooting and killing Nicki.

If Portman stands for the omnipresent, unpredictable danger of white hetero-patriarchy, and Frank stands for the ubiquity of the hetero-patriarchal white-savior complex, then Nicki could be cast as a homophobic interpretation of Robyn's position—the personal assistant—an opportunistic insider who secretly harbors villainous motivations.

But Fletcher's the one who truly resembles Robyn: physically, in boyish, soft-spoken demeanor—and figuratively, as the singer/actress's most stable attachment and most innocent bystander.

As Rachel, Whitney preenacted the stratospheric level of fame she'd achieve from the film; the soundtrack, for which she recorded six of twelve tracks, remains one of the top fifteen best-selling records and the number-one best-selling soundtrack in recorded history.

Also having preenacted the anxieties of motherhood, she would give birth to her only child, three months before embarking on the Bodyguard World Tour.

10.

Bobbi Kristina Brown was born in March 1993. Postpartum, Whitney brought Bobbi Kristina to family friend Aunt Bae, who provided early primary care for Bobbi Kristina; as Aunt Bae says in *Whitney*: "She slept with me in that bed wherever we were for the next eight years."

From the outset of their life together, Bobbi Kristina and Whitney's attachment formed a duplicate link in a familiar lineage.

Whitney's longtime friend and stylist, Ellin Lavar, says in *Whitney:* "In the beginning, she was a good parent. Whitney hated leaving Krissi. It's hard when you're working, when you're traveling. She had the same situation as her mom. But she insisted on taking Krissi on tour."

For the rest of her life, Whitney would repeat (to repair) the trauma of her foundational separation from Cissy—in a role reversal with Bobbi Kristina.

"All Kristina ever wanted was to have her mom's attention one-on-one, and the majority of the time that just didn't happen," Robyn writes in *A Song for You.* "It was primarily in the recording studio or during live performances that mother and daughter bonded."

For the rest of her life, Bobbi Kristina would always already miss her mother.

11.

Whitney's next leading role filmed from February to May 1995, and she recorded three new singles for its soundtrack, released in the winter of that year. Based on 1992's best-selling novel by Terry McMillan, *Waiting to Exhale* costars Angela Bassett, Loretta Devine, Lela Rochon, and Whitney—age thirty-two—in a group portrait of four best friends living in Arizona. Whitney's character, Savannah, exemplifies sober composure—the voice of reason and reassurance—as her sister figures undergo romantic turmoil. Paradoxically, Whitney experienced an overdose on set, causing a recess in production.

On the Bodyguard World Tour, Whitney's substance use had escalated. In *Can I Be Me*, Whitney's real-life bodyguard, David Roberts, says he filed a report to those in charge of Nippy, Inc., stating that drug dependency would lead Whitney to "destroy herself." In response, he was dismissed from the position. Overall, *Whitney* suggests that the staff of family and friends disregarded the singer's addiction in order to keep their jobs.

A Song for You depicts Bobby Brown's influence as the catalyst. Around this time, Whitney and Bobby's infamous marital trouble intensified—owing to his own substance use as well as his history of physical abuse. Robyn reveals that the spouses were quarreling while Whitney filmed *Waiting to Exhale*; she writes: "Whitney's character was Savannah, a television producer who, after years of believing the married man she's in love with will leave his wife, finally stops settling for the fantasy and learns to embrace her life without him. I hoped that Whitney would connect with this strong character and stand up for herself." But when Bobby visited Whitney on set, she overdosed.

Nevertheless, Whitney plays Savannah so convincingly, the discord of Whitney's psychological demons remains imperceptible in her delivery, while the central themes of her trauma pervade the plot.

Savannah moves to Phoenix for a new job. Bernadine, Gloria, and Robin live there—each at a momentous personal turning point—and they gratefully embrace the arrival of their stalwart friend. Bernadine's husband leaves her for a white mistress, and, in an iconic scene, she *protests* by emptying his closet into his car, dousing the clothes in gasoline, and, after lighting a cigarette, tossing a lit match on top. Gloria *despairs* when her ex-husband admits that he's bisexual, which throws her son into a homophobic tantrum: "My father's a queer!" he angrily chants in disbelief. And Robin dates a string of mean men before *detaching* from them to bear a child alone.

Savannah's dilemma: All the men to whom she attaches are attached to other women. And her mother, on the phone, nags her: "Every woman needs a man." Overly invested in Savannah's romantic interests, her mother is also financially dependent; mother tells daughter that her food stamps were revoked and that she has only sixty dollars, and daughter wires money to mother the next day. Over the course of the storyline, Savannah's either guarding her life-making around several irresistible yet unavailable men or rescuing her loved ones from their world-building breakdowns. Finally, Savannah accesses the courage to challenge her mother: "I'm smart, I work hard, and I'm a good person. Ma, if I allowed myself to think like you, I guess I'd be a dead woman."

Savannah abruptly hangs up, then calls back to apologize. Consolingly, her mother responds, "It's all right. I just don't wanna see you end up like me."

The film ends on a high note for everyone: The friends reach smoother plateaus, each having resumed relatively steady foothold in the ordinary. And this is revelatory. Because, unlike in *The Bodyguard*, Black power plays a prominent part in *Waiting to Exhale*. White hetero-patriarchy is personified by the mistress—"a white woman," as the friends refer to her—a destabilizing force that Bernadine eventually overcomes, achieving liberation from a controlling marriage. The mistress briefly appears in the film; she's meek, bland, blond. Bernadine slaps her face.

Directly contrasting *Waiting to Exhale*'s exaltation of attachment among women, this moment in Whitney's private life turned most aggressively homophobic toward Robyn. *A Song for You* recounts: In 1995, the ex-boyfriend of Whitney's former publicist told the tabloids that Whitney's father offered to pay him to break Robyn's arms and knees with a baseball bat. "I don't want her murdered. That would devastate Whitney," father allegedly told the middleman (John denied the accusation).

Robyn persevered—despite persistently dreading, she writes, "the threat of bodily harm."

12.

From January to May 1996, Whitney filmed her third and final starring role: *The Preacher's Wife*, costarring Denzel Washington. Whitney's character, Julia, provided the singer/actress both a return to her origins and an opportunity to cross genres: *The Preacher's Wife* soundtrack comprises fifteen gospel tracks recorded by Whitney.

In the opening scene, she exuberantly leads a church choir, under a child's voice-over: "That's my mom. The Lord blessed her with the gift of song. She's been singing in this church her whole life." The speaker, Jeremiah, is the son of Julia, the daughter of the church's previous reverend, and Henry, the church's current reverend. Jeremiah narrates as the camera centers on Julia's mother, Marguerite: "That's my grandma. Everyone says she needs a man." Julia holds the last note, and Jeremiah imitates her. Henry then delivers a lackluster rendition of Julia's father's old sermon, which Jeremiah imitates after the service, preaching to a snowman outside. Immediately, the central themes of Whitney's trauma pervade the plot—in Jeremiah's mimicking both his parents' gestures of religious faith and their notions of hetero-patriarchal normativity.

Henry's depressed; with his church in disrepair and strapped for funding, he alternately *detaches* from and *despairs* to Julia, whose prim disposition reinforces her husband's do-good reputation in the community. Henry prays for a savior. Dudley the angel drops from the sky. To start, Henry *protests* the intrusion, but Dudley eventually becomes Henry's confidant. Family romance arises when Henry grows too withdrawn and Jeremiah grows too fond of Dudley, who attempts to mediate with the sparring spouses while advising Henry in the best interest of the church's longevity. Then, Dudley grows increasingly fond of Julia. One night, he encourages Henry to take Julia out dancing at the jazz club where she used to sing, but Henry insists that Dudley take her instead. On the dancefloor, the club owner (played by Lionel Richie) invites Julia onstage. Here, she sings the soundtrack's hit single, "I Believe in You and Me," and it's

Whitney—age thirty-three—at her apex, skating across octaves with Olympic dexterity. Paradoxically, in 2009, Whitney told Oprah that around the time of filming *The Preacher's Wife*, she'd been using drugs heavily on a daily basis. Julia's persona distanced Whitney's persona from the abjection of addiction.

Julia and Dudley's attachment strengthens. Henry and Marguerite disapprove; indignant and territorial, Henry orders Dudley to leave. The expulsion of the angel—harmless adviser, helpful companion—uncannily prefigured an impending catastrophe of separation that hastened Whitney's downturn.

PART THREE

13.

Whitney's fourth studio LP, *My Love Is Your Love*, was released in November 1998—the title track featuring a vocal clip recorded by Bobbi Kristina, age five. Traveling on the My Love Is Your Love World Tour, in *Can I Be Me*'s archival interview footage, Whitney says:

> Bobbi Kris and I have a great relationship, we really do, and I'm very, very proud of that. I cherish it. And I am really dying to get home to see her little face, and she's dying for me to come home… I had her out here the first half, before she went to school. The day that she had to leave, I thought that we would be strong, I thought I would be strong and I wouldn't cry, but I couldn't help it, and I just really broke down, and she did, too. It made me feel really good—and I felt really bad because I knew I had to let her go—but it made me feel really good to know that she would miss me and love me as much as I missed and loved her.

Here, Whitney speaks to the simultaneous pleasure of attachment and torture of separation. It feels good to be missed as badly as one misses another.

And now, another torturous attachment-separation occurs. Near the end of the tour, Robyn abruptly departs from the entourage.

Can I Be Me emphasizes the conjecture of a journalist who frequently reported on Whitney, Alison Samuels: "I'm assuming [the family] paid her off. I don't know, but she just disappeared... I think they prevented it—I think they understood that [Robyn and Whitney] could not connect again—it had to be Bobby and Whitney and this family unit."

Whitney conveys a contradictory scenario: Robyn presented an ultimatum—lose Bobby or lose me—and Whitney responded, *I accept your resignation*.

Robyn, who declined to participate in both documentaries, discloses what truly transpired in *A Song for You*. Whitney skipped a recording session with George Michael in 2000, and Robyn sent him a gift to apologize on Whitney's behalf. When Robyn relayed the news to Whitney, Bobby verbally assaulted her: "You don't buy a gift for a man from my wife! Are you crazy?" Robyn writes:

> I understood exactly why I was getting blasted. They were strung out of their minds. There was nothing I could do to make things any better. I was no longer able to protect Nippy. I had done all I could do, and for the first time I realized that I needed to save myself.

Then and there, Robyn relinquished her position in Whitney's circuit of attachments. And indeed, weeks later, Robyn received a message that Whitney had accepted her resignation.

14.

The decade succeeding Robyn's departure unraveled with the discord of Whitney's psychological demons.

John assumed total control of his daughter's creative enterprise and, according to several interviewees in *Whitney*, embezzled her fortune. Whitney cut ties with him, and he filed a lawsuit for one hundred million dollars—claiming neglect, from his deathbed, on national television, two months before passing away, in February 2003.

Ellin Lavar says, this time in *Can I Be Me*: "I think the biggest change in her came when her dad disappointed her... She was secure in the fact that *Daddy's got my back, he's gonna protect me, he's gonna take care of me*, and when that trust was broken for her, it broke something inside of her that she could never repair."

Whitney portrays multiple battles in the upheaval of the singer's identity: private life versus public image, public image versus the world. In a segment of home-movie footage, she looks at the camera and says: "Whitney can call Nippy, but Nippy can't call Whitney."

Being Bobby Brown, a reality television show capitalizing on Whitney and Bobby's eccentric marriage, was filmed in 2004, aired in 2005, and canceled after eleven episodes. Then, Whitney and Bobby took to isolating at home in Atlanta, where their codependent drug use intensified, erupting in their 2006 separation and 2007 divorce. Over the subsequent five years—sporadically releasing records and appearing in the supporting roles of several films—Whitney cycled through rehab, sobriety, and relapse. Bobbi Kristina also struggled with addiction and codependency—as mercilessly sensationalized by the tabloids—while she aspired to a singing career of her own.

On February 11, 2012, the Beverly Hilton hosted a gala for the Grammy Awards, and Whitney, Bobbi Kristina, Cissy, and other family and staff members were lodging there in preparation to attend. Around 3:30 that afternoon, Whitney's assistant returned to the hotel suite and found the singer unresponsive in the bathtub. At 3:55—age forty-eight—Whitney was pronounced deceased.

In Fairview Cemetery of Westfield, New Jersey, her plot is alongside her father's.

Three years later, on January 31, 2015, at home in Atlanta, Bobbi Kristina was also found unresponsive in the bathtub. Following six months in a coma, she passed away that July, at age twenty-two.

In Fairview Cemetery, her plot is alongside her mother's.

15.

This can't wind down on that note. Instead, back to March 31, 1991, Easter Sunday, at the Naval Air Station in Norfolk, Virginia, where thousands of soldiers have gathered upon returning from the Gulf War. Three months earlier, Whitney sang "The Star-Spangled Banner" at the Super Bowl. Now, she's on a live broadcast for HBO (to be released on VHS as *Welcome Home Heroes with Whitney Houston*, then released on DVD as *A Song for You: Live*)—her first televised concert and first concert video.

Here, now—at age twenty-eight—she sings Leon Russell's tune from 1970, "A Song for You"; her lissome voice floats and dives across an oceanic range of tones and emotions. Accompanied by longtime collaborator Bette Sussman on keyboard and longtime bandmate Kirk Whalum on saxophone, Whitney rests on a cushioned barstool, center stage, her face glistening with sweat, one diamond stud in her right earlobe and one golden crucifix dangling from her left. Microphone in hand, she painstakingly incarnates a portentous farewell:

> *I love you in a place*
> *Where there is no space or time*
> *I love you for my life*
> *You're a friend of mine*

And when my life
When my life is over and done
Remember, remember, remember, remember when we
When we were together
'Cause now, now we're alone
And I am singing this song for you...

for Robyn, for her mother and her future daughter, for her father and her future husband, for her god.

Robyn recalls:

> I don't know why, but Nip decided to include "A Song for You" in that night's set list. It was the first time she performed it. In fact, it was the first time I heard her sing it. We'd listened to the song before... One night at our first apartment, we lay side by side on the floor, our heads propped on pillows, the only light coming from the stereo we faced. I selected The Temptations' "A Song for You," an album I treasured... I watched from the sound booth as she perched on a stool and belted the song, her own interpretation, which sounded to me like a plea. I never heard her sing it live again.

16.

The back cover of the 1985 vinyl edition of the debut *Whitney Houston* lists the singer's acknowledgments in a column along the right-hand side. It begins: *God grant me the courage to accept the things I cannot change, the things I can, and the wisdom to know the difference.*

It ends: *Robyn, What an assistant! I love you and I guess all you need to do is stay in my life.*

Three decades later, this then-innocuous, now-ominous warning prefigures the homophobic severance of a crucial attachment, which would contribute to the identical demise of a mother and her only child.

POSTLUDE

When I entered daycare, I met my first best friend, D—also one of my very first playmates, since I am an only child. For a decade, we were inseparable. By coincidence, D lived in my school district, and so we also attended the same rural public school, containing roughly four hundred elementary, middle, and high school students in one building, where he was one grade below me. D's sister, N—two grades above me—became part of our widening circle of friends who, on summer breaks, went to a YMCA day camp for preteens. There, one day, D passionately persuaded me to accept our mutual friend's proposal to be my first—and only—girlfriend. Even then, I'd intuited that, for D, this acceptance would disprove my obvious queerness and reify the illusion of our relationship's heteronormativity.

D and N's mother would drive the three of us to the Y's gymnasium to catch the bus to the campgrounds, and my mother would pick us up from the Y at the end of the day to drive home. On those rowdy bus rides from the gym to camp and back, D and I always sat together. There, one day, his baseball cap slipped under the seat in front of us. As he bent over to retrieve it, I was so moved by my affinity for him that I spontaneously expressed it through a fatal gesture: I placed my hand on his backside. I must've been nine; he would've been eight. Bolting upright, he unraveled—he detected no trace of affection in my touch—he detected transgression. From that moment onward, he denied my apologies, explanations, peace offerings; he refused my attachment.

Following the incident, N grew old enough to supervise D on schooldays off—which became the case for many of my friends and their siblings. Deprived of their companionship at camp and day-off programs, I gradually learned to survive my terror of solitude: I'd sublimate my discomfort by listening to music—pacifying those horrendous hours of dread of abandonment by flipping the cassettes of *The Bodyguard*, *Waiting to Exhale*, and *The Preacher's Wife* soundtracks in my Walkman over and over. There, I found faith in Whitney's faith—her acts of devotion, her voice of conviction—I identified with her need to believe, not yet aware of the demons (family romance, separation anxiety, addiction) we'd end up having in common.

Throughout middle and high school, N and I remained friends, despite the complications of my being attached to someone whose sibling became increasingly homophobic and hostile toward me. During N's sophomore, junior, and senior years, she lived with osteosarcoma, a cancer in the bones. For three years, our friends and I helplessly witnessed her sickness and treatment, her multiple remissions and recurrences. For three years, we endured an agonizing impending separation: our youngest, most intimate encounter with premature dying and death. The last time I saw N, after her graduation party, she drove me home in the dawn, and we sat in her car in my driveway, discussing our futures. That summer, she passed away.

I still miss my friends.

MARIAH, FIONA, JOANNA, AND ME

On My Vocabulary

One day, I realized the loneliness of love and needed to tell some-one—but had no one to tell. I wrote it down. Ever since, I've been fishing for words—reeling in phrases and tossing them back into the sea of love's lonely missives, traumatized, gasping for breath.

There, on the shore of the sea of love, like a stone house, I've weathered the elements.

"What does that mean?" I'd ask my mother whenever I encountered an unfamiliar term, and my mother would define it succinctly. One day, I asked what the word *gay* meant, and she told me, "It's when two men or two women fall in love and hold hands."

Even then, I sensed some strange shame in saying the word *love*. As an early reader, I'd pretend not to know how to read "love"—pausing for the adult to read the word instead. Even then, this compulsion to speak succinctly and free of shame. Still, now, saying "love," my tongue swells at the edges of the *L*, my throat swallows the *O*, my teeth timidly touch the *V*, my lips stiffen and cower with a tail between the *E*.

Still, now, this compulsion to speak succinctly and free of shame. During a poetry workshop in graduate school, a professor criticized my poems for containing an abundance of adjectives and adverbs. "Nouns and verbs are stone," they told me. "Adjectives and adverbs are just mortar." Well, the way I see it, you can't build a stone house without mortar.

"What does that mean?" I've asked time and time again. I'll never stop asking—never stop grasping for surprising and inevitable adjectives and adverbs to precisely elaborate my precious nouns and verbs. It's life's work.

From earliest memory, I've exhibited an unusual dexterity for memorizing song lyrics. I can recite entire career-spanning catalogs of lyrics—including those of most of the musicians named within this book. In chronological order, Mariah Carey, Fiona Apple, and Joanna Newsom all had the profoundest influence on my vocabulary. What follows isn't a comprehensive account of the terms that I strongly remember learning from their songs (if it were, words like *stentorian* would appear under "Fiona" and *ululate* under "Joanna") but a compendium of those that I use—to this day—to interpret the world.

1. MARIAH

Apprehension
Blatant
Disillusion
Elusive
Emblazoned
Euphoric
Hectic
Incessantly (my friends and I invented a nonsense phrase to replace
    this word in the song "Heartbreaker"—"in Cecily" is how we
    sang it—until I learned the correct word and told all my friends)
Indefinitely

Inevitably
Liberated
Nonchalant
Obscure
Rapture
Relinquish
Resounding
Sacred
Subconscious
Succumb
Suppressed
Unyielding
Vividly

2. FIONA

Abide
Abound
Appeasing
Carrion
Coercion
Cryptic
Demeanor
Deride
Deviant (adjacent but not quite equivalent to the word *deviate*, which
    recurs throughout this book—along with variations of nearly
    half the terms on this list)
Discern
Endeared
Endeavor
Enrapture
Fondle
Harrowing
Imbue

Inversion
Manifest
Oblige
Oblivion
Paramour
Redeemed
Undulate

3. JOANNA

Bolt upright
Clambering
Dolorous
Hale
Indiscreetness
Keening
Inchoate
Inflammatory
Lissome
Lordly
Neverdoneing (technically, not a real word—nevertheless, an
    adjective that I use to describe a delay, a prolonging)
Stone fruit

NEGLIGENT MOMS
On Cher

1. OVERTURE

Jackie Jean Crouch was a few weeks shy of twenty years old in May 1946, when she delivered her firstborn, Cherilyn, in El Centro, California.

Born in Arkansas, Jackie Jean had started singing at age five, busking for coins with her twenty-six-year-old father on guitar as they made their way to California to pursue a music career. In Los Angeles, at age thirteen, Jackie Jean found work as a housekeeper, and by May 1946, she'd made her way to El Centro. As a new, single mother, Jackie Jean was earning three dollars per twelve-hour shift at an all-night diner before she found a singing job at a bar-and-grill, earning seventy-five dollars a week. In order to save that money, she left Cherilyn in the care of a Catholic orphanage, where she was encouraged to give up the child for adoption. But Jackie Jean returned with Cherilyn to Los Angeles, delivered a second child, Georganne, and became an aspiring actress known as Georgia Holt.

At age eighteen, Cherilyn recorded the song "Ringo, I Love You" under the moniker Bonnie Jo Mason, then recorded a single,

"Dream Baby," as Cherilyn. That same year, 1964, she released a handful of singles with her romantic partner, Salvatore Phillip Bono, as Caesar & Cleo. That September, their first hit, "Baby Don't Go," was released under yet another moniker: Sonny & Cher.

2. BEST SUPPORTING ACTRESS

Two months after Sonny & Cher's "I Got You Babe" reached number one on the *Billboard* Hot 100, in October 1965, Cher released her debut solo album: *All I Really Want To Do*, billed as Chér (note the acute accent mark over the *e*). Imperial Records's official bio read: "Cher, who has just turned 19, had seemed more destined for an acting career than one in music. Her mother has been acting in Hollywood for a number of years and started Cher off on a dramatic career a few years ago... It has only been in the last year, working diligently with Sonny, that Cher has come into her own as a vocalist."

As a vocalist, Cher went on to release eleven commercially successful solo LPs, from 1965's debut to 1973's problematically titled *Half-Breed*, swiftly reaching the stellar status she retains today. Her mother told *Ladies' Home Journal* in 1975:

> My father lived long enough to see Cher become a star. We sat together when she appeared at the Hollywood Bowl. He kept telling me, "That's you up there, Jackie, that's you!" I loved my father dearly. He had tremendous drive to be a somebody, to accomplish things. He never did. But I always told myself I was somebody—even when I cried myself to sleep as a maid.

And so, mother's dramas of identity and career created a ripple effect in the identity and career of her child, who, as an actress, would repeat those dramas: on the surface—on film—and behind the scenes, with her own children. Cher's imminent shift from singer to actress would not only revive her livelihood and renew her celebrity, it would also provide crucial creative space where she could attempt to repair these formative traumas.

*

In March 1969, Cher delivered her firstborn: a female-bodied baby, who Cher and Sonny named Chastity, who'd later transition to become a man named Chaz.

The child's namesake, a film called *Chastity*—written and produced by Sonny—premiered in June 1969 and featured Cher in her earliest lead role, as a bisexual hitchhiker trying to outrun the trauma of sexual abuse. The film flopped—so did "Chastity's Song (Band of Thieves)," a single recorded by Cher for the film. Her label, Imperial, dropped her.

Following public separation from Sonny in 1974—and the birth of her second child, Elijah (fathered by Gregg Allman), in 1976—through to 1982, Cher released six consecutive commercially unsuccessful solo LPs, and her singing career took an unsteady track.

A single mother of two, she needed a more stable job.

*

February 1982: Cher debuted on Broadway in Robert Altman's production of a play by Ed Graczyk, "Come Back to the Five and Dime, Jimmy Dean, Jimmy Dean." The show's limited run received lukewarm critical attention; nevertheless, Altman adapted it as a feature film in November 1982—also starring Cher, in the same role—which Pauline Kael reviewed in that month's issue of *The New Yorker*: "Moving in apparent freedom, the principal actresses go at their roles so creatively that, I think, they've found some kind of acting truth in what they're doing... 'Truthful' acting may be affecting to us because it represents the sum total of everything the actors have been affected by. It comes from areas far below conscious technique; it's true to their psyches."

Impressed by Cher's performance—which earned her a nomination for a Golden Globe: Best Supporting Actress—Mike Nichols cast her in 1983's *Silkwood*, as Dolly, the queer roommate of Meryl Streep's lead character. Cher won a Golden Globe for this role: Best Supporting Actress. Written by Nora Ephron and Alice Arlen, the screenplay was also nominated for an Academy Award—along with Cher, for Best Supporting Actress.

3. *MASK*

Rusty Dennis was born Florence Tullis in Brooklyn in 1936. In 1961, in Glendora, California, she delivered her second child: a son named Roy Lee, nicknamed Rocky. Born with craniodiaphyseal dysplasia—a rare bone disorder of excess calcium deposits on the skull, which leads to distortion of facial features (also called *lionitis*)—Rocky had a head that grew twice larger than average, and his prognosis was declared fatal from his diagnosis at age two until his death at sixteen. Rusty sold the rights to Rocky's story for fifteen thousand dollars. In 1985, novice screenwriter Anna Hamilton Pheelan's script became a twelve-million-dollar production by Peter Bogdanovich, with Rocky played by Eric Stoltz and Rusty played by Cher.

Cher portrays Rusty as a single mother barely balancing her erotic relationships alongside her responsibilities for Rocky. Fiercely protective of her son, she challenges and defeats the male characters (her boyfriends, his doctors, the high school students and faculty) who attempt to victimize him because of his appearance. But her desire for drugs often overrides her devotion to him. Drugs make her irritable and impatient—preoccupied when Rocky tries to connect—to the point that he brings home from school a stack of pamphlets on chemical dependency prevention. One night, she's especially short-tempered as he attempts conversation while she gets ready to go out. Imploring her to stay home, he smashes a dinner plate as she moves for the door; he shouts, "I hate you going out all the time and coming home wasted out of your mind!" They argue, heatedly; defeated, child says to mother, "All you care about is getting loaded. And laid." Mother slaps child on the face.

This slap catalyzes *Mask*'s turning point, which occurs the next day: Rocky and Rusty attend a carnival, where her dealer offers her drugs and she declines. Rocky enters a funhouse and encounters his reflection in the funhouse mirror. The warped image displays his face as it would appear without disorder.

*

Jacques Lacan's "The Mirror Stage" scrutinizes the *imago*, the transformation that's initiated the instant that the infant identifies itself in its reflection. Lacan suggests that, in this moment, "the mirror-image would seem the threshold of the visible world." The self, recognizing itself, situates itself within space. "The *mirror stage* is a drama," Lacan continues, "which manufactures for the subject, caught up in the lure of spatial identification... the armor of an alienating identity, which will mark with its rigid structure the subject's entire mental development." This armor (flesh, fat, muscle, bone) creates the shape that one grows to know oneself to be—the shape that one grows known by others to be—and its appearance determines one's advantages and disadvantages in dominant society, where one is evaluated by others against certain standards of normativity.

Rocky's encounter with the funhouse mirror transpires immediately after Rusty refuses her dealer, as though mother's drug abuse had prohibited son from perceiving himself as independent of his disorder. The mirage of normalized facial features allows him to complete a postponed mirror stage. As Lacan concludes: "This moment in which the mirror-stage comes to an end... decisively tips the whole of human knowledge into mediatization through the desire of the other…" In the mirror, in the mind, the "I" learns to see itself in its shape. Then, the "I" yearns to see itself through the eyes of others. And so, romance enables the continuation of Rocky's identity formation, allowing him to break the barriers of his self-loathing—the result of having been evaluated as disabled for his unique appearance. Working at a summer camp for blind students, Rocky meets a blind peer named Diana (played by Laura Dern), who becomes his first girlfriend. When Rocky returns home from camp, he learns that Diana's parents have forbade their relationship. Shortly thereafter, Rocky passes away in his sleep.

"Rusty Dennis is played by Cher as a complicated, angry, high-energy woman with a great capacity to love her son and encourage him to live as fully as he can," wrote Roger Ebert, in 1985. "[She] makes Rusty Dennis into one of the most interesting movie characters in a long time." Cher won Best Actress at the 1985 Cannes Film Festival and received a nomination for the 1986 Golden Globe— Best Performance by an Actress in a Motion Picture – Drama—but *Mask* was otherwise overlooked by major awards. However, the gravity of the role further legitimized Cher's acting career and advanced her image as both irreverent rulebreaker and unconventional mother figure.

Mask's subject—the tyranny of appearance, the pressure placed particularly on perfecting one's face—mirrored a theme that would pervade public discourse around Cher's public image for the ensuing decades. During a 1984 interview with Terry Wogan, Cher admitted to having undergone cosmetic surgery—revealing that even her mother had recently received a facelift—and the topic was a tabloid spectacle by the time of Cher's November 1990 *Vanity Fair* cover profile, "Starred and Feathered," wherein she bemoaned: "I don't know why people are preoccupied with my cosmetic surgery… It mystifies me that people would care what I do to my body." This statement presages another drama that would transpire between mother and child in Cher's future personal life.

4. *MERMAIDS*

Following *Mask*, Cher acted the lead in three consecutive films, all departing from the role of mother figure.

- *The Witches of Eastwick* (1987), as part of a trio (with Susan Sarandon and Michelle Pfeiffer) wielding their newly discovered magical power, seduced by the devil in disguise (Jack Nicholson)

- *Suspect* (1987), as a public defender assigned to represent an unhoused, hearing-impaired veteran (Liam Neeson) wrongly accused of murder

- *Moonstruck* (1988), as a widow romantically embroiled with her new fiancée's brother (Nicholas Cage), for which she won that year's Academy Award for Best Actress in a Leading Role as well as a Golden Globe for Best Performance by an Actress in a Motion Picture – Comedy or Musical

Then, her LP of 1989, *Heart of Stone*, featured her touchstone hit "If I Could Turn Back Time."

Cher's dual careers were cohering, and she resumed an upward track.

From September to December 1989, she filmed *Mermaids*, cast as Rachel: single mom to Kate (Christina Ricci) and Charlotte (Winona Ryder), whose voice-over refers to the eccentric matriarch as "Mrs. Flax." As in *Mask*, *Mermaids* depicts the mother's motivation for sex and romance as negligence, and the damaging consequences of her impulsive distractions are begrudgingly endured by her maladjusted children.

In her opening scene, Mrs. Flax sings along to Peggy Lee's "Fever" on the radio as she picks out a dress for a date, wearing a black negligee and pink kimono. Kate (devoted to competitive swimming) and Charlotte (devoted to Catholicism) watch TV. Mrs. Flax serves them a makeshift dinner before rushing out to her date (her married boss), who honks from his car. Then, with the POV above the parked car, which rhythmically rocks in a parking lot, Charlotte's voice-over declares: "That means we'll be moving soon." Earlier, she'd declared that the family had already relocated eighteen times—presumably, whenever one of Mrs. Flax's romances failed. Now, inside the car, panting from kissing, Mrs. Flax's boss breaks off their affair. Mother and children pack their station wagon and relocate to Eastport, Massachusetts.

Thus, *Mermaids* plots the course charted by a mother's erotic entanglements, trailing her children in its wake. Mrs. Flax's amorous decisions will eventually engender Charlotte's amorous decisions, which will ultimately endanger Kate's well-being.

Mother and children move to a house neighboring a convent, and Charlotte's instantly infatuated with the convent's caretaker, Joe—a shy, handsome high school graduate. Mrs. Flax nurtures a flirtation with Lou, the owner of a shoe shop. As Charlotte's desire for Joe grows isolating, Mrs. Flax's irreverent candor—and focus on Lou's courtship—alienates Charlotte and estranges Kate.

The turning point is set in motion following John F. Kennedy's assassination. "I miss my father. I wonder if he's watching television," says Charlotte's voice-over, as she wanders among dazed, devastated crowds gazing at the news on TVs in storefront windows. Joe rings the convent's bell. Charlotte climbs to the top of the bell tower, comforts his grieving, and kisses him—her first kiss. Seized by guilt, she abruptly absconds. Ashamed of her indiscretion—and afraid of immaculate conception—she steals her mother's car and escapes to New Haven, Connecticut, where she spends the night with a wholesome nuclear family of four, regaling them with fables about her (imaginary) benevolent father.

Mermaids constructs its drama behind a veneer of comedy, ambivalent to its protagonists' crises of faith and fidelity. The emphasis on this unexpectedly grave sequence surrounding JFK's assassination underscores the grieved absence of patriarchal care that would ostensibly enhance the lifestyles of mother and children. The film's overall premise proposes that Mrs. Flax's and therefore Charlotte's motivations are propelled by the pursuit of proximity to paternal men. Kate (innocent, infantilized, almost androgynous), the swimmer, attempts a different but perhaps analogous pursuit: underwater immersion.

When Mrs. Flax attends a New Year's Eve costume party as a mermaid, she and Lou argue about their uncertain future, and he defeatedly leaves alone at midnight. Joe gives Mrs. Flax a ride home, and in the driveway, she kisses him. The child watches her mother with her lover from the front window. "You kissed her?!" Charlotte shouts in disbelief. Mother, amused, mocks child.

This kiss—mother's rivalrous betrayal of child—instigates the forthcoming catastrophe at the climax.

*

On an individual's earliest form of kissing—thumb-sucking—Freud offers, in *Three Essays on the Theory of Sexuality*: "Thumb-sucking is determined by a search for some pleasure which has already been experienced and is now remembered... It was the child's first and most vital activity, [the] sucking on [the] mother's breast, or at substitutes for it, that must have familiarized [the child] with this pleasure."

To Freud, this fundamental act, in part or in whole, compels people to kiss—to pursue the gratification instilled by nursing in infancy. Thumb-sucking "makes [the child] independent of the external world, which [the child] is not yet able to control," Freud suggests. "At a later date, [the child] seeks the corresponding part—the lips—of another person. ('It's a pity I can't kiss myself,' [the child] seems to be saying.)"

The pleasure—the independence and control—of Charlotte's kiss becomes usurped by the pleasure, independence, and control of Mrs. Flax's kiss.

*

The night after kissing Joe, Mrs. Flax goes out, and Charlotte puts on her mother's black negligee—sucking an unlit cigarette, staring at herself in the mirror—singing "Fever" while choosing a dress. Applying lipstick, Charlotte brags about kissing Joe, telling Kate that kissing another person can be like "kissing your hand" or "kissing yourself in the mirror."

The sisters drink wine from their mother's jug. The convent bell rings, and the sisters stumble over to the bell tower. Charlotte climbs to the top, finds Joe, and has sex for the first time.

Meanwhile, hiccupping, Kate collects rocks by the creek and drunkenly falls in, overtaken by the current. The nuns rescue her, and she's rushed to the hospital. Later, with Kate in recovery, Mrs. Flax rages at Charlotte and instructs her to begin packing. Charlotte smashes a dinner plate in protest, begging to stay and finish high school.

"What's your major, town tramp?" Mrs. Flax asks.

"No, Mom, the town already has one."

Mother slaps child on the face.

The climactic scenario in *Mermaids* is identical to that in *Mask*: mother slapping her child's face, both injuries prompted by child insulting mother's lifestyle—"loaded and laid" in *Mask*, "town tramp" in *Mermaids*—and both insults accompanied by the child smashing a dinner plate. Because each mother reacts with such offense, maternal pleasure is tacitly stigmatized. Mother decides that she doesn't identify as a hedonist. And yet, in both *Mask* and *Mermaids*, slaps set in motion uplifting denouements: Rusty's sobriety and Mrs. Flax's reconciliation with Charlotte. Inflicting physical harm in reaction to their children's insubordinate language, the characters Rusty and Mrs. Flax no longer recognize themselves.

At the end of *Mermaids*, mother and daughter bond over Mrs. Flax's loss of Charlotte's father and Charlotte's loss of Joe, who moves to California. Mother says to daughter: "You know, you're just one year younger than I was when I had you. If you hate my life so much, why are you doing your damnedest to make the same mistakes?"

Now, her performance most authentically embodies Pauline Kael's idea of acting truth—the "sum total of everything the actors have been affected by"—because the role rings so true to Cher's psyche.

And in fact, her 1990 *Vanity Fair* cover profile reads: "Cher's new film, *Mermaids*, is a warped tribute to her mother, Georgia Holt, a perennially aspiring singer and actress…"

Here, Georgia tells the reporter: "When I saw *Mermaids*, I went, 'Jesus Christ, is that the way I did with my children?'… And Cher says, 'Mother, do you know how many times you made us move?' But I was always trying to move us to a better place."

5. FINALE

At age thirteen, Cher's firstborn, Chastity Bono, privately identified as gay but didn't come out to the family until age eighteen. After being publicly outed at twenty-six, Chastity became a prominent activist for gay rights. In 2008, at age thirty-nine, Chastity commenced the process of gender transition, changing names to Chaz in 2010.

The 2011 documentary *Becoming Chaz* lovingly chronicles his experience, including his hormone treatments and bilateral mastectomy. Chaz confesses that he'd disliked being photographed and filmed in the past, because he'd hated his body since puberty. Post-operation, Chaz looks at his new chest—in a mirror—on camera. He's ecstatic.

Also post-op—before seeing his mother in person—he watches the interview footage that she recorded for the documentary, where Cher confesses:

> I was hysterical one day because I was calling Chaz's answering machine, and I realized it was her old voice. And then I said, "Chaz, is there a way I can save it? Because I will never hear that voice again." And there wasn't. And it was gone. For me, that's the most traumatic thing that's happened to me in the whole thing is, like, hearing her voice and knowing I'll never hear it again.

As a queer icon, Cher confronts her transphobia, which creates an edifying subplot in the documentary; it portrays an ordinary mother reconceiving her perception of gender norms, in reconciliation with her own preferences—for instance, the statement she'd made in *Vanity Fair*: "I don't know why people are preoccupied with my cosmetic surgery… It mystifies me that people would care what I do to my body." Ultimately, she accepts the idea of gender affirmation, because she so adamantly self-identifies with being female—and could imagine, being male, desiring transition herself.

Cher initially resisted but eventually accepted Chastity's homosexuality; likewise, she gradually respected Chaz's transition, finally acknowledging him through masculine pronouns live on David Letterman's show, which Chaz watches in real time during the documentary—the second scene wherein Chaz witnesses his mother vocalize her revelations about his gender identity on television.

Dear Mom, Love Cher, the Lifetime TV feature of 2013, contains intimate interview footage of Georgia Holt and her two daughters. Georgia recalls tableaus from her own childhood—singing for money to feed herself and her father—as well as her short-lived acting career and her six marriages. She even recalls an episode from Cher's childhood, when daughter stole mother's car—a scene reminiscent of Charlotte's joyride in *Mermaids*.

To coincide with the TV feature, Cher remastered Georgia's song recordings from the 1980s and released the LP *Honky Tonk Woman*—Georgia's debut country album, at age eighty-six—including a mother-daughter duet, "I'm Just Your Yesterday," which they perform together at the feature's end, their contraltos strikingly similar.*

"What do you think about the fact that we sound so much alike?" asks Cher.

"Well, I think that's kind of natural," Georgia responds.

6. ENCORE

I remember, at age five, noticing my mother's likeness to Cher's portrait on her self-titled LP of 1987, which I owned on cassette and would play over and over in a boom box alone in my bedroom. I also owned the VHS tapes of *CherFitness*, her duo of aerobics videos, which I'd follow as a daily workout regimen alone in the living room. There, on the sofa, during my sexually frustrated early childhood (when I'd sublimate this frustration by French-kissing my fist or forearm), I'd routinely rewatch *Mask* and *Mermaids*, looking to the

---

* After I wrote this, Georgia Holt passed away—in Malibu, California, on December 10, 2022. On December 13, Cher posted to Twitter/X: "Look for Cher & mom sing 'I'm just your yesterday.' You'll see where I stole my voice."

unapologetic eroticism of Rusty and Mrs. Flax as examples of the possibility for sexual fulfilment. These films were such fundamental facets of my identity formation, their scenes are as familiar to me as my face in a mirror.

Cher was my mother when my mother was too busy at work, too consumed by homemaking, too distracted with separating from my emotionally abusive father. But I recognized that my mother was not Rusty or Mrs. Flax—because she did not prioritize her needs over mine; she sacrificed a lot of freedom in order to fulfill the role of primary caregiver. This role necessitated her working relentlessly, maintaining the house and property, even forsaking romantic opportunities. And so, I did recognize Rusty and Mrs. Flax in the behaviors of some of my mother's friends—as well as in some of my friends' mothers' behaviors. This is how I learned to appreciate the generosity of my mother's caregiving style: by noticing the ways in which it contrasted with the more negligent styles of those others.

BLACK IS THE COLOUR OF
MY TRUE LOVE'S HAIR

On Nina Simone

Nina Simone's live album of 1970, *Black Gold*—a recording of a concert at New York's Philharmonic Hall on October 26, 1969—opens with a solo piano arrangement of the folk ballad "Black Is the Color of My True Love's Hair" (with "colour" spelled in the British style on the album's track list). Here especially, Nina's androgynous timbre radically subverts the division between masculine and feminine pitch—the vocal range impossible to categorize without a visible body.

The singer croons and warbles, as though confessing a secret; that the true love, who is called "he," has black hair suggests that another, more legitimate but less preferable lover's hair is not black—a clandestine desire.

Halfway through the seven-minute performance, Emile Latimer plucks his guitar. Nina rejoins on piano, and an androgynous timbre continues to croon and warble, now regarding a true lover who is called "she."

For years, I'd thought that Nina had switched pronouns, and I'd wondered why the recording hadn't provided sufficient evidence of her clandestine queerness. But in fact, the singer of this track's latter half is Emile Latimer, whose voice sounds indiscernibly similar to Nina's.

Now, if the listener doesn't register this switch in vocalists, then Nina addresses both pronouns. Disembodied, the voice has unfettered choice of gender to embody and desire.

IS LANGUAGE A VIRUS?

On Laurie Anderson

1.

Laurie Anderson's song of 1986, "Language Is a Virus (from Outer Space)," takes its title from a dubious allusion to William S. Burroughs. After the first year of the COVID-19 pandemic—a year marked by fears of contagion and isolation—in my paranoia and alienation, I became obsessed with locating the phrase's exact source.

The track was released as a single to promote Anderson's concert film, *Home of the Brave*: a compilation of several video recordings from New Jersey's Park Theater in 1985. The multimedia show featured charming, androgynous Anderson singing, reciting spoken word, playing violin and keyboard, and dancing acrobatically, accompanied by more than a dozen fellow musicians and vocalists—including an appearance by Burroughs himself.

Anderson hadn't been important to me until this moment in 2021, as the novel coronavirus continued to afflict every aspect of our society with the threat of disease and death. One of the lone remedies available then, before a vaccine had been developed and made more accessible: face masks, to cover the nose and mouth—because the virus transmits by way of the salivary droplets and aerosols that we emit while we breathe and speak. Speaking to someone remains a particularly fraught experience; to this day, I picture droplets and aerosols—my own and those of others—floating between our faces. I picture our droplets and aerosols dispersing through open windows and doors. When strangers approach, I exhale all the way to the end of my breath and hold there. I don't inhale until we're six feet away again.

Watching *Home of the Brave* in 2021, I was struck by how the performers' costuming looked so apropos of the moment—their heads covered by hazmat-style balaclavas; hands sheathed in sterile white gloves; limbs cloaked in matching lab coats, jumpsuits, and business attire. Coinciding with the film's debut in 1986, a music video aired on MTV, featuring a different instrumental arrangement, which would be released as the single, and alternate concert footage. Here, the performers wear the same suits, gloves, and balaclavas—their bodies entirely enveloped in various fabrics, save for their exposed mouths.

To open both the concert film and music video, the projection of a quotation attributed to Burroughs reads: "Language is a virus from outer space."

2.

This quotation is attributed to Burroughs, verbatim, in various online outlets—but with either an incorrect citation or no citation at all.

Burroughs also hadn't been important to me until 2021, when the prospect of literary sleuthing invigorated my sense of purpose in a moment of limited prospects and dwindling purpose. I scoured Burroughs's books, intent on pinpointing the exact source that inspired Anderson's song. Doing so would've solved one trivial mystery among the multitude of more consequential mysteries, but to this day, I haven't been able to identify the text.

In the closest phrasing that I could unearth, Burroughs begins the essay "Ten Years and a Billion Dollars" by writing: "My general theory since 1971 has been that the Word is literally a virus." He elaborates: "The Word clearly bears the single identifying feature of virus: it is an organism with no internal function other than to replicate itself."

Language does "go viral," online, on television, on the radio; ideologies transmit at rapid speeds across airwaves, phone lines, cell sites, and wireless routers—communication being communicable—infecting, infiltrating, inciting human bodies to act and react.

3.

Anderson uses the phrase in question when, in the lyrics' narrative, the narrator hears someone utter the sound *ugh*, which the narrator's companion calls *a pain cry*.

The narrator responds: "Pain cry? Then language is a virus."

This non sequitur makes for a somewhat clumsy and mystifying segue. What renders a pain cry as evidence of language's virulence?

4.

Anderson doesn't use the phrase "from outer space" in the song lyrics proper.

And I haven't encountered the word *virus* anywhere near the term *outer space* in Burroughs's books. In his novel *Nova Express*, "word dust drifted from outer space"—but the word isn't necessarily virulent there. It's rather benign; word dust drifts in the malignant light of "a million drifting screens" throughout the city—a sort of Times Square at the end of the mind, where words litter the gutter and screens reign supreme.

Seventy minutes into the ninety-minute *Home of the Brave*, Burroughs's silhouette appears from behind a blue scrim (the contours of his fedora, a dead giveaway) before he appears in the flesh, a martini in his left hand and a cigarette in his right, to deliver a thirty-second monologue: the intro to "Sharkey's Night"—their collaborative track on Anderson's LP of 1984, *Mister Heartbreak*.

Burroughs's participation implies that he must've sanctioned Anderson's use of the quotation. And further, in interview footage attached to the music video on YouTube, Anderson states explicitly: "This is a quote from William Burroughs. 'Language is a virus from outer space.'"

5.

Still determined to find the quotation verbatim, I sent a message to Ira Silverberg—a friend and colleague to me and to Burroughs as well as the coeditor of *Word Virus: The William S Burroughs Reader*—to ask if he knew where it may be located. He recommended either "Electronic Revolution" or *The Ticket That Exploded*. Both Burroughs texts replicate the concept of the "word virus"— but neither yielded Anderson's phrase.

"You know his redundancies are numerous," Silverberg wrote back.

Language mutates.

6.

If language is a virus, does it spread on surfaces?

My lover tells me that language wouldn't live, would be dormant and inactive, without the human—the host—to write and read, say and hear, sign and see it.

Any language left unexpressed when I die dies, too.

7.

For over a decade, I've loved this language from *A Lover's Discourse* by Roland Barthes: "Language is a skin. I rub my language against the other."

A virus is a skin: a shell of proteins or lipids encasing DNA or RNA. Viruses purportedly compose 8 percent of human DNA. Is a human a virus?

If we imagine language as a virus, then it's possible, Burroughs's *Nova Express* imagines, to "rub out the word forever."

I'm rubbing my language, like a salve, against this surface.

8.

I don't think that language is a virus. A virus is not a metaphor.

A virus ravaged human bodies around the world as I rubbed out these words. And I rubbed out these words because my life depended on it.

Because language isn't a virus, language is a remedy (and we're already out in space).

HOP ALONG;
OR, THE PRONOUN "THEY"
On Frances Quinlan

1. FRESHMAN YEAR

Early in 2022, recently separated from my partner of ten years, I needed to find consolation in something new but somehow simultaneously familiar.

I hadn't listened to Hop Along since 2009, when the band went by the name Hop Along, Queen Ansleis—at that time, the solo project of Frances Quinlan, a vocalist, rhythm guitarist, and visual artist based in Philadelphia who studied at the Maryland Institute College of Art and started performing and recording original songs around 2005. In 2005, during the spring semester of my freshman year at SUNY Purchase, my new friends and I would play on a loop a track called "For the bonsai tree u bought 4 me," which was available exclusively via Hop Along, Queen Ansleis's MySpace profile. Frequently, I'd hear its melody from down the hall on my way toward the open door of their dorm. *I'm a lonely parakeet, I have no home*, we'd shout with Frances, whose breathtaking voice and nimble-fingered guitar blasted from the speakers of our laptops in these temporary lodgings.

Frances self-released Hop Along, Queen Ansleis's sole LP, *Freshman Year*—burned on CD-Rs, packaged in photocopied paper sleeves—in August 2005, and it became the soundtrack to my sophomore year at Purchase. On a frigid night that winter, Frances came to play a set at the "co-op"—a coffeehouse-style health food store attached to the dining hall, where students could put in shifts for work-study credit. One of my few drunken memories at the show involves my perching on an amplifier to be nearer to Frances, then shouting the entirety of "The Goose and the Wren"—right down to the incidental asides and background vocals of the rendition on *Freshman Year*. That night, my friends and I planned a party at their on-campus apartment, and we invited Frances, who accepted—and whom I photographed there, hand over heart, standing against the wall where we'd stuck 3D foam letters spelling out HOP ALONG. We even played a favorite *Freshman Year* track that Frances hadn't performed—"Hi Too Loo Rye"—blasting it from an iPod hooked up to cheap speakers and shouting in unison, which humiliated us all. One of my final memories—and one of my final moments—at Purchase involves driving my station wagon around the traffic loop that encircles the secluded campus for the last of countless occasions, with *Freshman Year* blasting from the car speakers and all four windows rolled down, shouting these lyrics from "For Sebastian, from a Friend": *Hop along, sing your song, your guidance counselor was wrong!*

Throughout the thirteen years that I didn't listen to Hop Along, Queen Ansleis, Frances released three LPs under the name Hop Along—joined by bandmates Joe Reinhart (lead guitar), Tyler Long (bass), and sibling Mark Quinlan (drums)—and then, under the name Frances Quinlan, the singer-songwriter/guitarist released *Likewise*, a solo LP, in 2020. In 2021, Frances began using "they" as their preferred pronoun. And around 2022, so did I.

2. IS SOMETHING WRONG?

Frances's voice can be, together or in alteration, dulcet and strident, reedy and clarion—a clarinet and a cornet.

They tend to sing in a shout, singed with "vocal fry," which happens when the larynx is contracted, causing the vocal folds to slacken. This yields a loose closure in the glottis, allowing air to escape, which creates a low-frequency popping and sizzling quality. The phenomenon goes by numerous names—glottal rattle, glottal scrape, creaky voice, laryngealization—as well as the German term *Strohbass*, or the straw bass (I imagine four strands of straw plucked as strings on an upright bass: a dry hiss and crackle). Technically the lowest register of a human voice, vocal fry ranges below the modal register, or the average speaking voice.

Possibly the most-cited demonstration of vocal fry is Britney Spears's *oh baby, baby* from "... Baby One More Time." Merely one of innumerable incarnations, it has come to overrepresent vocal fry—and to characterize stereotypes of the so-called valley girl and the queer-voiced man—thereby stigmatizing the sound, perhaps for being a marker of hyper-femininity. In the early 2010s, news media from *The Atlantic* to *Business Insider* reported that vocal fry proved detrimental to women in the job market. More recent studies have approached vocal fry at a generous—albeit obliviously gendered—angle; for instance, in 2016, the Acoustical Society of America's paper "Why Vocal Fry?" reported: "When female singers use this lowest register, listeners rate her as more expressive... The opposite is true for men."

But to describe Frances's voice, I wouldn't say *feminine*, and I wouldn't say *masculine*. I wouldn't say *androgynous*, either. I would say *child-like*—in that the timbres of children can sound similar, regardless of gender, prior to puberty. (But I wouldn't say *prepubescent*.)

Music journalists have attempted—by comparisons to other singers and through eccentric metaphors—but have failed, as I fail now, to accurately encapsulate Frances's tone and technique. Jesse David Fox's excellent profile of Frances for *Vulture* in 2015, "Is This the Best Voice in Rock Music Today?," speaks to the sound, calling it "the rasp, which [Frances's] brother and bandmate Mark speculates showed up when [Frances] had to start being louder than [Mark's] ex-metal-band-member drums." (On the contrary, I detect Frances's rasp developing as far back as *Freshman Year*, before Mark joined the band; though the rasp could be adjacent to the "death growl" of a heavy metal singer.) Fox compiles a litany of descriptions from past Hop Along reviews and even asks friends to contribute their own comparisons and metaphors, such as: "If *Pablo Honey* Radiohead were super into *In Rainbows* Radiohead and Thom Yorke were a woman with strep throat."

I nod to this description in particular because it underscores the vocal gender line—which, more often than not, underscores the overall perception of a person and their sound. This description also nods in the direction of vocal fry, as it affects the larynx; strep throat affects the pharynx.

Ultimately, it may be pointless to describe a voice—or any sound—in an age like today's, with the audio available so freely online. Here, I'm driving at this point: I initially encountered and perceived Hop Along as music made by a female-bodied singer-songwriter/guitarist, but now I am reencountering Hop Along as music made by a nonbinary singer-songwriter/guitarist, and I have not experienced a significant shift in my perception of this person and their sound. In fact, "they" clicks into place when I think and speak of Frances—the way I wish "they" would click into place for those who think and speak of me.

In the heat of one of our final disagreements, my partner of ten years claimed that it was difficult to speak of me using "they" after having used a gendered pronoun for as long as we'd known each other. This is the same argument my mother uses regarding one of my cousins, who also prefers the pronoun "they." I believe this argument disguises latent homophobic and transphobic tendencies, which can consciously or subconsciously prevent someone from earnestly attempting to reconceive of another's gender expression. But I digress—at least, for the moment.

Preceding Frances and the band's debut LP as Hop Along, two EPs were released in 2009: *Is Something Wrong?* and *Wretches*. I stopped listening after *Is Something Wrong?*—and only lately started listening to *Wretches*. One sultry summer night in 2008, Frances played a solo set at ABC No Rio, and I recorded, on a cheap digital camera, several of the seven songs that would later compose *Is Something Wrong?* Over and over, I'd listen to the (regretfully long-lost) footage—my own private bootleg. *Is Something Wrong?* also circulated on CD-Rs, packaged in photocopied paper sleeves, and my only access to it currently relies on a YouTube playlist that, with constant low-grade anxiety, I fear may also disappear someday before I remember to extract the audio and save as MP3s. For safekeeping, a lyric from the opening track, "Junkyard James," I shout: *Queen Ansleis is about to jump.*

3. GET DISOWNED

To digress once again, I will address what I call "guitar catharsis." Having established the pointlessness of describing a sound, I urge you, if you're able, to listen to the beginning sixteen seconds of "Tibetan Pop Stars," the second track on Hop Along's official debut, *Get Disowned*—here, one of innumerable incarnations of guitar catharsis.

A working definition of *catharsis* may be helpful. Professionally, I'm partial to *Merriam-Webster*'s dictionary, whose primary entry for the word reads "purification or purgation of the emotions (such as pity and fear) primarily through art." Guitar catharsis occurs when the tenor of the guitar or guitars can enunciate—and therefore purify or purge—an emotion that can't be conveyed by the human voice or vocabulary.

Following the self-release of those two EPs in 2009 and prior to the debut of *Get Disowned* on Hot Green Records in 2012, guitarist Joe Reinhart joined Hop Along. A founding member of the band Algernon Cadwallader, Joe—who also recorded and mixed *Get Disowned*—remains, to my mind, the major orchestrator of Hop Along's exceptional propensity for guitar catharsis.

Don't get me wrong, Mark's drumming contributes immensely to the music's cumulative cathartic effect; the drumming articulates a profound shared language that only siblings can coinvent. However, contradicting Mark's belief that Frances's vocal fry originated in relation to the drums, I believe that it became more pronounced in relation to additional guitars: Frances utilizes the technique not to vocalize louder than the volume of the drums but to vocalize the textures of guitar catharsis.

Joe graduated to lead guitarist with Hop Along's sophomore LP, *Painted Shut*. Beforehand, on *Get Disowned*, Frances and Joe were joined by guitarists Dominic Angelella on a few tracks, Peter Helmis (also from Algernon Cadwallader) on one track, and Nick Bockrath on another. The substantial difference between *Freshman Year* and *Get Disowned*—and the substantial difference between *Is Something Wrong?* and *Wretches*—exists in the volume of guitars: from Frances's lone acoustic to layers and layers of guitars overlaying Tyler Long's intuitive and apposite bass.

Coincidentally, Dominic Angelella, who also played guitar on *Wretches*, joined Lucy Dacus's band on bass, and in July 2022, Hop Along opened for Lucy Dacus at SummerStage in Central Park—the first Hop Along show I'd seen since 2018. By July 2022, I'd been ardently listening to Hop Along again on a daily, daylong basis for about six months—and living alone for seven. That scorching evening at SummerStage—so scorching, the event staff sprayed hoses of cold water on us sweating spectators—Frances utilized not only extra vocal fry but also much rubato in order to be heard above and across the shouting-along of numerous zealous fans. And the guitar catharsis was almost more intense than I could endure; "Tibetan Pop Stars" made me weep vehemently, purging and purifying my post-separation self-pity and fear, tears streaming from behind my sunglasses.

"I think Hop Along is too punk for me," I heard someone exclaim, departing the crowd after Frances left the stage.

As I neared the exit, an event staff member raised an eyebrow and remarked, "Lucy Dacus is about to go on."

I responded, "I was here for Hop Along."

4. PAINTED SHUT

Hop Along's Tiny Desk Concert of 2015 on NPR, which I didn't watch until 2022, moved me to reconsider their repertoire. Presenting three songs from the sophomore LP, *Painted Shut* (released in 2015 by Saddle Creek, who'd reissue *Get Disowned* the next year), the Tiny Desk set starts with "Horseshoe Crabs," wherein Frances sings from the perspective of a male speaker: Jackson C. Frank, a folk musician who recorded one gorgeous, gut-wrenching self-titled LP in 1965. The authenticity of perspective in "Horseshoe Crabs" could easily be mistaken for Frances's own autobiography, and this is a prominent facet of their brilliance: They skillfully embody the emotions of outside characters, to achieve personal catharsis. The subject of *Painted Shut*'s "Buddy in the Parade," Charles "Buddy" Bolden, was a cornetist and forebear of jazz, and by means of Buddy's biography,

Frances achieves (in my estimation) the most cathartic moments on the LP.

As far back as *Freshman Year*, Frances shifted between gendered positions through their lyrics. The speaker of "Hi Too Loo Rye," for one, awakes in the body of "an old man" named Stanley Forbes. Although I'd suspected the title character of "Elizabeth & Elizabeth" had been one of the songwriter's former romances, the singer embodies the speaker of "Bruno Is Orange" to such an authentic extent that I'd pined for a romance resembling the one I'd imagined Frances had experienced (and may have actually experienced) with someone named Bruno: *That boy is an armed man, bearing flowers and two hands*—which, for eighteen years, I'd misheard as "bearing flowers *in* two hands. Nevertheless, because Hop Along lyrics usually focus on friendships more than romances—and because these lyrics usually relate various characters' narratives from an omniscient viewpoint—the genders and sexualities of the speakers remain largely immaterial.

Mid-June 2022, with "Horseshoe Crabs" playing on a loop in my mind, I met someone—a new romance—who I'd eventually photograph bearing a bucketful of homegrown flowers in both hands, just like in my mishearing of Frances's Bruno. At that SummerStage show in late July, preoccupied by this new romance and processing it by repetitively listening to *Painted Shut*, I also wept vehemently during their performance of tunes off that album—especially "Well-Dressed," which had been second in the Tiny Desk set. That night, I filmed a clip of "Well-Dressed" on my iPhone and sent it to my new romance.

But the last time I'd gone to a Hop Along show, at Brooklyn Steel in May 2018, I left before the end of the set. I'd joined an old friend from Purchase with whom I hadn't connected in as long as I hadn't listened to Hop Along, and I think we'd both hoped that an element of nostalgia would provide some common ground. Alas, we'd grown as unfamiliar as the newfangled songs being performed by our once favorite band—whereas the crowd of zealous fans appeared excessively familiar, shouting along and superseding Frances—while I felt preoccupied with worrying about my partner, who was waiting at home, so I fibbed an excuse to leave early.

"Did they play any old ones?" I later messaged my friend, who messaged back, "No, only new ones."

5. BARK YOUR HEAD OFF, DOG

Looking at the setlist of that Brooklyn Steel show now, I know I would've appreciated the performance to the utmost—had I been able to see it after a year of reacquainting with Hop Along. More than half the set comprised tunes off their third and most recent LP—*Bark Your Head Off, Dog*, released by Saddle Creek in 2018—and, indeed, comprised no tunes older than those from *Get Disowned*.

Fittingly, the final line of "Sister Cities," the final track on *Painted Shut* (as well as third and final in the Tiny Desk set)—*I had to shoot that dog you loved so much*—becomes reincarnated in the title of the following LP. This sort of reincarnation reverberates within Frances's discography—from figures such as dogs and bears, cousins and parents, to entire songs: *Freshman Year*'s "Laments of a Mattress," for one, was revamped with drums and additional guitars and retitled "Laments" on *Get Disowned*.

Mid-December 2022, Hop Along headlines a show at Brooklyn Made, with Dominic Angelella as the opener. Tonight, Frances plays an old one: *Freshman Year*'s "Bride & Groom Hot Air Balloon," which had been revamped with drums and additional guitars—featuring Dominic Angelella—and retitled "Bride & Groom" on *Wretches*. Tonight, Dominic joins Frances onstage for "Bride & Groom," (And tonight, it's "Laments" that makes me weep vehemently.) During "Prior Things"—the final track on *Bark Your Head*

Off, Dog—when Frances sings a line that mentions their parents' backyard, I look at Mark, whose facial expression contains pain and joy synchronously, revealing the composition and its performance to be uniquely cathartic for both siblings.

Tonight, I overhear people in the crowd refer to Frances by the feminine pronoun, and it strikes me as discordant. It stings. Then, while the band banters between tunes, Mark refers to Frances as "they," and it clicks into place: melodic, utterly organic, as though Mark has been thinking and speaking of Frances this way all their lives.

Finally, tonight, someone repeatedly requests a song from *Wretches* called "Second Name" (also known as "Second Voice," as the person requesting it calls out)—an eleven-minute track alluding to Frances's changing of their given name—but Frances demurs. A few months later, "Second Name" will become my anthem, as I finish working on these words.

"I've come to understand (better) why I felt so compelled to start going by my middle name when I turned 18," Frances announced via Twitter/X, on January 22, 2021: "I needed distance from a role that I have never understood or felt agency within… Identifying as nonbinary has helped me to finally be at home in this body. The pronouns they/them feel most right to me."

6. LIKEWISE

Despite our past disagreement, at present, my preferred pronoun sounds most organic in the voice of my former partner—one of the few people who consistently respects my preference—who tells me it's in my power to demand such respect. And yet, I've created alienating scenarios for myself and others in voicing this demand. I don't disidentify with the masculine pronoun ("I'm not *no longer* 'he,'" I've taken to explaining), but when used in reference to my person, it strikes me as discordant. It stings. Quite frequently, my loved ones refer to me by the masculine pronoun and then bashfully self-correct, generating further discord. On the few occasions when I've corrected my loved ones, I've regretted the punitive dynamic that results. So, for the time being, I've stopped patrolling the way others think and speak of me. Rather, I've chosen to lead by setting an example: eliminating gendered pronouns from my vocabulary as often as possible—indicating people by name or structuring syntax that doesn't depend on gendered pronouns, thus using them intentionally and not automatically.

Likewise, released by Saddle Creek in January 2020 under Frances's full chosen name, signaled an intentional shift in tone and technique. While still featuring instrumentals by Joe, Tyler, and Mark, these compositions decenter the guitars and drums and instead center around piano, organ, synthesizer, violin, cello, and harp—all present on Hop Along albums, particularly *Bark Your Head Off, Dog*, but in much smaller measure. Consequently, Frances utilizes remarkably less vocal fry—their pitch far more dulcet than strident. To my ear, the most pronounced instance of vocal fry can be heard on "Went to LA"—a song intended for *Bark Your Head Off, Dog*, according to *Rolling Stone*'s March 2020 feature on *Likewise*. This latest endeavor both deviates and advances from Frances's nearly twenty-year precedent; until their next endeavor, it provides the starkest evidence of the artist's relentless pursuit of self-discovery.

By extension, throughout the majority of thirteen months, I traced Frances's evolution, commencing with *Freshman Year* and leading to *Likewise*—forward, backward, then forward again—and along this trajectory, I found myself consoled by something new and somehow simultaneously familiar.

COLORS OF THE WIND

On Pocahontas

1.

During the first year of the COVID-19 pandemic, in the midst of a state-mandated lockdown—quarantined in an apartment built on the land once known as Lenapehoking by the Leni Lenape tribe, renamed Breuckelen by Dutch colonizers, and now known as Brooklyn, New York—I watched and re-watched Disney's *Pocahontas*.

At age ten, I'd sung "Colors of the Wind"—the theme song of *Pocahontas*—into the microphone of a boom box and recorded myself on a blank cassette tape. That day, when I played the recording, I was humiliated to hear—effeminate inflection, nasal vowels, slight lisp—a queer voice. Queerness was still beyond my comprehension then, but I intuitively understood the sound could be considered dissonant from my gender presentation, and so, it struck me as embarrassing. Of hearing my own voice, this is my earliest memory.

2.

At age ten, the historical figure we call Pocahontas experienced mere traces of the events depicted in the Disney animation of 1995.

Born circa 1596, named Matoaka, renamed Amonute, and nicknamed Pocahontas, she's believed to have been the daughter of Powhatan, the chief of about thirty American Indian tribes living in the area then known as Tsenacommacah, where England colonized Jamestown, Virginia.

Disney dramatizes a romance that didn't truly transpire between Pocahontas and English captain John Smith. In reality, beyond the timeline encompassed by the movie (but loosely portrayed in its sequel), Pocahontas married John Rolfe, a tobacco plantation owner, in 1614—following her capture by the Jamestown colonists, conversion to Christianity, and baptism as "Rebecca." In 1616, she traveled to London—where she was presented to the royal court as an example of an American Indian who'd been successfully "civilized"—and there, in 1617, after contracting tuberculosis, she passed away before she could return home.

The earliest record of Pocahontas's existence appeared in *A True Relation of Virginia*, published in 1608 by the real-life John Smith, who'd joined the Virginia Company, chartered by James I, to build settlements along what we now call the North American coast. The animation depicts Smith as debonair as any Disney protagonist— blond-haired and blue-eyed—voiced by Mel Gibson (who was, at that time, an American sweetheart, not yet known for his ultraconservatism). In reality, John Smith appeared rugged—his portrait at the National Portrait Gallery engraved with bristly beard and furrowed brow, his statue at Jamestown National Historic Site cast as squat and thickset—and he had a reputation for antagonism; en route from London, the ship's captain charged him with mutiny and sentenced him to execution, but owing to Smith's dexterity for exploration, his life was spared and he became instrumental in the establishment of the colony.

Smith's *True Relation of Virginia* reads: "Powhatan understanding we detained certain savages, sent his daughter, a child of ten years old, which not only for feature, countenance & proportion, much exceedeth any of the rest of his people, but for wit, and spirit, the only Nonpareil of his Country." Chief Powhatan had sent Pocahontas, Smith writes, as "a token of peace" to "beg the liberty" of the Powhatan tribe members in Smith's captivity. (And while no records exist concerning a romance between Pocahontas and Smith, he certainly emphasizes her physical appearance—her "feature, countenance & proportion"—here.) Nearly four hundred years later, the Disney musical would embellish and distort this encounter between these two historical figures.

3.

Throughout the summer of 2020, I bicycled to Washington Square Park for a weekly queer reading group called "Down with Rainbow Capitalism," organized by femme and nonbinary comrades who run a socialist publication called *Left Voice*.

We'd sit in two or three circles of five or six people—amplifying to be heard above our cloth, surgical, or N95 face masks—and we'd discuss texts that analyzed the intersecting inequities among class, race, gender, and physical ability. At the crux of each conversation: how capitalism created the conditions for classism, racism, sexism, and ableism—by continually deploying class, race, sex, and ability as categories in economic competition. For the comrades, the struggles against racism, sexism, and ableism were inseparable from the struggle against capitalist exploitation—and true queer liberation, only possible in synchronicity with the liberation of all people oppressed under capitalism.

I spoke seldomly, as shy about projecting my queer voice (even in a queer-friendly space) as I was scared of projecting my salivary droplets and aerosols in the pre-vaccine days of a viral pandemic. I listened a lot.

One of the comrades, who'd frequently wear a T-shirt bearing the phrase FUCK CHRISTOPHER COLUMBUS, once said something along the lines of: *What the colonizers considered "savagery" was the queerness of tribal society.*

There, I began to understand that the same Eurocentric, patriarchal, racist, religious, and capitalist apparatuses that had colonized the land and imperialized the tribes of Tsenacommacah, Lenapehoking, Mannahatta—where we sat—and all across this so-called country were the same apparatuses that had instilled the homophobic hatred of my own voice in me.

But can I juxtapose these narratives without paternalizing the history?

4.

Irene Bedard was twenty-seven in 1995, when she recorded the speaking voice for Disney's Pocahontas. Born in Anchorage to an Alaskan mother of Iñupiat and Yup'ik descent and a French Canadian father of Cree descent, Bedard made her screen debut in 1994, in the lead role of the made-for-TV movie *Lakota Woman: Siege at Wounded Knee*, as the real-life Mary Crow Dog. That same year, she starred in Disney's live-action *Squanto: A Warrior's Tale* as the title character's wife. In 1998, she voiced Pocahontas again for the straight-to-video *Pocahontas II: Journey to a New World*. And in 2005, she performed the role of Pocahontas's mother in Terence Malick's live-action *The New World*.

Bedard's 60-plus film and television credits typecast her as the avatar for several of the 574 federally recognized Indian Nations—homogenizing the portrayal of culturally diverse tribes through the "feature, countenance & proportion" of one person: one of *People* magazine's "50 Most Beautiful People" of 1995. While these roles amounted to a prolific career for Bedard, they inadvertently precluded a spectrum of possibilities for representation (say, a performer of Lakota descent playing the lead in *Lakota Woman*).

Bedard had studied musical theater at Philadelphia's University of the Arts—and later pursued a career as a singer; in 2003, she sang in a band and recorded an album with her husband at the time, musician Deni Wilson. But she didn't provide the vocals for Pocahontas's singing. Pocahontas's singing was recorded by a white vocalist named Judy Kuhn.

5.

Pocahontas serenades John Smith with "Colors of the Wind" in their earliest scene together, which is illustrated as a chance encounter that develops into a kind of first date. At the crescendo of Smith's patronizing flirtation, he refers to Pocahontas and the Powhatans as "savages" (as does the real-life Smith, in his actual account)—and she rejoins in song. Now, Judy Kuhn takes over for Irene Bedard. The melody starts: *You think I'm an ignorant savage...*

Stephen Schwartz, the soundtrack's lyricist, writes on his website: "In the song, I basically wanted Pocahontas to address the Eurocentrism of John Smith; so in essence, it's a consciousness-raising song." Still, among all the source material I've read in reference to "Colors of the Wind," no one acknowledges the Eurocentrism of hiring a white vocalist for an American Indian character—especially with a trained singer already voicing the part.

Quite the contrary: Kuhn has been perennially celebrated for her contribution—for instance, in 2019, Alan Menken, the score's composer, said in an interview with Playbill Presents: "There's an earthiness to her voice that I think fits Pocahontas." Then, the introductory verse plays in the background: *You think I'm an ignorant savage...*

Kuhn's rendition won a Grammy, Golden Globe, and Academy Award for best song, while a rendition by Black vocalist Vanessa

Williams reached the top ten of several *Billboard* charts; Williams's recording plays as the movie's credits roll—and omits the introductory verse.

"The verse that takes you to the song proper," Judy Kuhn said, in the same interview with Playbill Presents, "I always think of the verse as the kind of bridge from speaking—whatever the drama of the scene is that leads you to need to sing—the lyrics to that intro: It's sort of the challenge, it's sort of throwing down the gauntlet."

The gauntlet of the song proper takes its shape from an alleged speech and/or letter delivered by Chief Seattle, the head of a Duwamish tribe in the area we now call Puget Sound, responding to an offer to purchase his territory. On Schwartz's website, he cites Chief Seattle's words as the lyrics' inspiration—and incorrectly cites those words as having originated in a letter to Congress—while, in the Playbill Presents interview, Kuhn incorrectly cites a White House speech. In fact, the now-discredited belief was that Chief Seattle addressed the governor of Washington State in 1854, expressing bewilderment at the concept of purchasing and owning land. The supposed address was transcribed by a Duwamish-speaking English poet and published in 1887 in the *Seattle Sunday Star*. Another belief holds that Chief Seattle wrote a letter to President Franklin Pierce in 1855, expressing the same bewilderment. However, key details have been widely disputed by historians, and original documents haven't been located, so the National Archives declared the validity of both legends "very likely spurious."

6.

In 1616, John Smith wrote a letter to Queen Anne of Denmark, announcing Pocahontas's visit to London: a letter that describes—and, scholars believe, exaggerates or even fabricates—a scene depicted in numerous engravings and paintings, and which Disney depicts at the movie's climax. Smith claims he was detained by

Powhatan and brought to execution—but Pocahontas (then age twelve or thirteen) "hazarded the beating out of her own brains" to rescue him, purportedly sparing his beheading by shielding his body with her body. Elaborating his claim in *The Generall Historie of Virginia, New-England, and the Summer Isles*—published in 1624, seven years after Pocahontas passed away—Smith wrote, in the third person: "Pocahontas the Kings dearest daughter, when no intreaty could prevaile, got his head in her armes, and laid her owne upon his to save him from death."

Disney recasts this tableau thirteen minutes from the movie's conclusion. Following Pocahontas's recital of "Colors of the Wind," her clandestine romance with John Smith takes on a Romeo-and-Juliet quality. One night, they abscond to the woods, trailed by both a compatriot of the Virginia Company and the tribe member who Pocahontas's father intends for her to marry; the former shoots and kills the latter—while Pocahontas and Smith finally kiss—and the tribe brings Smith into custody, where the doomed romance takes on a Christ-and-Magdalene quality. Then, thirteen minutes from the end, during a crucifixion-style ceremony, Chief Powhatan lowers his club toward Smith's skull and Pocahontas rushes in to sacrifice herself for her paramour. "If you kill him, you'll have to kill me, too," she says. "I love him, father."

This seemed profound to me, at age ten, holding my Pocahontas action figure and harboring my John Smith fetish; after all, she confesses forbidden desire (queer love) to her father, which inspires him to declare peace with his enemies.

And so, in 2020, curious about this human who's been surrounded by so much fallacy, I compared the fabled episode as it appears in two popular biographies.

My affinity began in ignorance—and intensified the closer I got to the facts.

7.

Pocahontas: Medicine Woman, Spy, Entrepreneur, Diplomat by Paula Gunn Allen elaborates the episode the way it most plausibly would've occurred, determining that the ceremony may have been a symbolic adoptive ritual, wherein Chief Powhatan could've strategically formed an alliance with Smith—who probably misinterpreted the proceedings, owing to his misunderstanding of the Powhatan language. Deciphering Pocahontas's self-sacrificial gesture, Gunn Allen elucidates the "mother right" sociopolitical structure, "in which identity and inheritance derive through the maternal line"; she writes:

> Among the Powhatans, women had a deciding say in national policy and action. They also owned the great fields of corn, squash, beans, and other staples. They distributed all food and goods, including what was garnered by men in hunting and fishing. They designed and built the dwellings and the lodges for gatherings. It was natural and logical for the Gift of Life and Death to be bestowed on a woman.

While it's possible that Pocahontas performed an emblematic role in a traditional ceremony, the material conditions of the mother-right structure contradict the Eurocentric and patriarchal fantasy of the power relations crowning what we think we know of the Disney princess.

Similarly, *Pocahontas and the Powhattan Dilemma* by Camilla Townsend approaches the episode from a skeptical angle, explaining that Chief Powhatan may have symbolically adopted Smith to preserve political power, but a mock execution wouldn't have been performed in such a ceremony. Regarding the question of whether Pocahontas participated in the ritual, Townsend determines, "the answer is unequivocally no." Further, regarding Smith's initial account of Pocahontas in *A True Relation of Virginia*, Townsend asks: "Was she really the one then closest to Powhatan's heart, and did he believe that Smith would know this from his days of captivity and thus recognize her presence as a white flag? Or was she, as the daughter of a commoner and without claims to political power, among the children he could most afford to lose, and thus the one whose safety he chose to risk?" The Disney movie imagines that Pocahontas's mother had passed away long ago—her father thus portrayed as a widower. According to Townsend, in reality, Pocahontas's father was polygamous—and her mother's family not politically significant. The likelihood that the birthright of Pocahontas approximated the status of a Disney princess further diminishes.

But we can't know anything for certain. "She is visible only in the comments left by the white men who knew her and wrote down their impressions," Townsend concludes. "The problem is exacerbated by the fact that Pocahontas's language is largely lost… Thus we cannot even gain insights into Powhatan categories and assumptions by studying texts in their own language." On that note, Townsend conveys a heartbreaking detail from John Smith's log of Powhatan phrases: "'In how many daies will there come hither any more English ships?' was the very first full sentence Smith recorded. *Casa cunnakack, peya quagh acquintan attasantasough?*"

8.

Ultimately, I am one of those: a white, male-bodied person writing in English, launching conjectures and drawing conclusions through my exploration of those antiquated comments and impressions. And yet, here, I'm attempting to illuminate both the personal and historical implications of Disney's Eurocentric, patriarchal, racist, and capitalist influences on young viewers such as myself.

During the summer of 2020, in Washington Square Park, I began to understand that the origins of my attractions, my aversions, and even my indifferences could be traced from my childhood living room to the offices of the production companies that had been, were then, and still are manufacturing the heterosexist and white supremacist standards of normativity in American media. As an impressionable youngster, assembling my identity based on the authority of icons and moving images, I calibrated my value system to match the value systems that I witnessed on-screen.

At age ten, I admired Disney's Pocahontas because I wished to be desired by a man. Because queerness was still beyond my comprehension, I wished to become a woman, so I could engage in normative romances with men. Pocahontas's ostensible empowerment—as heroine, as martyr—drew me to her, and I imitated her in song. And in that song, I despised my voice.

9.

Subconsciously, I'd internalized my homophobia by absorbing Disney's homophobia.

The queerest character in *Pocahontas* is the villain: Governor John Ratcliffe, who leads the Virginia Company (in reality, he captained a different ship and became president of Jamestown colony). In the movie, he's animated as an eccentric, rotund, pink-and-purple-clad xenophobe who pillages the earth for gold. And his assistant, Wiggins—a dainty, dandyish, submissive yes-man—is voiced by the same actor. Even Ratcliffe's dog, Percy, is a fussy, effeminate male pug, who fosters an antagonistic flirtation with Meeko, the androgynous racoon. Thomas, a meek, juvenile company member, also codes queerly; he's inexperienced with a rifle, which he repeatedly misfires and then holds at crotch-level, ashamed. It's Thomas who shoots Pocahontas's suitor, Kocoum, on that fateful night, setting the climax in motion. And on that fateful night, Ratcliffe leads the Virginia Company in a flagrantly gratuitous musical number, "Savages," wherein they sing the word *savages* twenty-six times—an overture to the near-execution scene. After Pocahontas rescues Smith, Radcliffe shoots at Chief Powhatan and Smith takes the bullet. The queer villain endangers the figure of American Indian power, enabling Smith, the hetero-patriarchal white savior, to usurp Pocahontas's act of self-sacrifice with his bravery.

Within the wonderful world of Disney, at best, queerness equals comedy, naivete, and inferiority—mocked in contrast to valiant, nevertheless toxic, masculinity; at worst, queerness equals greed, pollution, and depravity. These standards of normativity provided my foremost exposure to displays of personal and interpersonal conduct, and so, my foundational codes of conduct—my attractions, aversions, and indifferences—were formed by adhering to this inherent and subliminal heterosexism and homophobia.

10.
But I'm learning to find affection for my queer voice.

And I've said enough for now.

Now is the time to listen.

AFTERWORD: B-SIDES & RARITIES

B-sides are virtually obsolete. Named for their location on vinyl records and cassette tapes, these tracks appear on the flip side of the single featured on side A.

B-sides typically became rarities, because they're often otherwise unreleased.

For instance, a B-side by Cat Power titled "Schizophrenia's Weighted Me Down"—a cover medley of Sonic Youth's "Schizophrenia" and Skip Spence's "Weighted Down (The Prison Song)"—appeared on the single for "Nude as the News" (from the LP of 1996, *What Would the Community Think*), which I discovered by surprise a few years ago, after a decade of considering myself an expert on Cat Power's entire catalog. I stumbled across the track on iTunes, where it's been available to download for a while, but the official upload to YouTube didn't post until January 2020.

Before the advent of YouTube—when message boards and torrent websites occasionally sourced the more obscure files—MP3s of B-sides could be difficult or impossible to obtain. Countless hours of my youth passed in pursuit of such rarities; the queerness of their obscurity enticed and enthralled me.

Through my fanatical searching and jubilant finding, I sanctified these MP3 files—assembling them into playlists and "burning" them on blank CDs that I christened with a Sharpie: *B-Sides & Rarities*—my personal music history compelled by their lore and allure.

This book couldn't have existed without the influence of certain singers—and certain B-sides—that almost didn't make it into this book.

1. JEWEL

In eighth grade, I was a runner-up in a poetry contest judged by Jewel—for my poem, "Sad Boy," an obvious imitation of the lyrics to Jewel's song "Fat Boy" from her sophomore LP of 1998, *Spirit*. Jewel's book of poetry, *A Night Without Armor*, published in 1998, had been a major inspiration for my writing poems, and from my earliest days of using the internet, I'd collected Jewel's demos, unreleased outtakes, and bootlegged rarities—many of which recently appeared as bonus tracks on 2020's twenty-fifth anniversary edition of her debut LP, *Pieces of You*.

By the time of Jewel's debut, B-sides were beginning to phase out; one-sided CD singles replaced cassettes and vinyl, and so, the US edition of Jewel's single for "Foolish Games," released in 1998, featured only its title track. However, the Australian and German editions contained two bonus tracks—one titled "Everything Breaks."

I didn't hear "Everything Breaks" until 2002, when the audio leaked from the live recording that would be her first concert film, 2004's *Live at Humphrey's by the Bay*. Here, Jewel's still a down-to-earth bohemian—not yet an out-of-touch megastar—and so, profoundly relatable to sixteen-year-old me.

Alone, perched on a wooden barstool in my living room, I played the recording through stereo speakers—lip-synching along, with an untuned guitar on my lap; I'd clamp the fret in my left hand and inaudibly strum my fingers on the right, as though performing at a coffee shop on open-mic night. This feigned singing accomplished so much catharsis—keeping such adolescent loneliness and boredom at bay.

The rendition of "Everything Breaks" attached to the *Pieces of You* twenty-fifth anniversary edition—which is, I surmise, the "Foolish Games" bonus track—differs in its tenderness from the intensity of the Humphrey's recording, as does a third and even tenderer rendition recorded for Jewel's LP of 2015, *Picking Up the Pieces*, where she repurposed several additional rarities.

As I revisit these three renditions today, the Humphrey's recording retains the original intensity that I'd tried to imitate.

Now, I clamp a phantom fret in my left hand and strum phantom strings with my right. I lip-synch the lyrics I remember.

2. JONI

After hearing Joni Mitchell's voice for the very first time, I sobbed myself to sleep. I must've been ten or eleven. *Blue* played in the background of an antique train car that had been parked on a concrete plot and converted into a bar and restaurant. Late one night, I sat there in a booth beside my mother, across from her friends; they swooned as *Blue* started, and it played (we stayed) to the end. Haunted by Joni's mournful tone, I wept from the parking lot to bed at home.

In 1968, Joni wrote (and recorded in 1969) a song called "Urge for Going." Intended to be on 1971's *Blue*, it became the B-side on her single of 1972, "You Turn Me On, I'm a Radio" (from her LP of the same year, *For the Roses*), then it was rereleased as the opening track of 1996's compilation, *Hits*.

I'd learned its lyrics before I'd heard its melody. "Urge for Going" appears as the leading entry in *Joni Mitchell: The Complete Poems and*

Lyrics—published in 1997—which I gifted to my mother for her birthday; my awareness of the book somehow predated my awareness of *Hits*, which would soon be widely available for purchase at Starbucks counters alongside its counterpart, *Misses*.

This phenomenon of learning lyrics prior to hearing their melody (and vice versa: knowing a melody prior to comprehending its lyrics) recurs in my personal music history. The culmination of this process—finally knowing both at once—resonates with the ecstasy of an infant who is finally able to verbalize: to form words out of sounds, to make meaning out of music.

3. ANI

No singles—and therefore, no B-sides—reside in Ani DiFranco's discography.

The closest semblance to a single: her EP of 2000, *Swing Set*—a six-track complement to 1999's *To the Teeth* (the cassette that inaugurated my Ani DiFranco collection). *Swing Set*'s two primary tracks: the radio edit and album version of "Swing"—a song from *To the Teeth*—which render this EP a single de facto, and by default, the remaining four tracks resemble B-sides.

Following a remix of *To the Teeth*'s title track, three covers close *Swing Set*: the first, a live cover of Woody Guthrie's "Do Re Mi." Back in my days of Ani, I was better acquainted with the singer's live cover of "Do Re Mi" on the compilation *'Til We Outnumber 'Em: Songs of Woody Guthrie* (released in 2000 by Ani's label, Righteous Babe Records). Here, Ani incorporates a snippet from *The Sound of Music*'s "Do-Re-Mi"—reinterpreted ominously—and the overall tenor of this performance sounds far more ominous than its already foreboding iteration on *Swing Set*.

On Guthrie's record of 1940, *Dust Bowl Ballads*, the speaker of "Do Re Mi" warns the listener that they won't succeed in California if they don't have the do-re-mi—the dough, the cash—or the cachet, as I interpret it: the cunning and courage necessary for survival in the cutthroat culture of post-Depression migration from the Midwest to the West Coast. Guthrie's innocent, optimistic tenor—his sweet warble, his upbeat guitar—suggests that his persona tells this cautionary tale because he *doesn't* have the do-re-mi, and so, he's going back to where he came from.

Ani's gutsy, cynical spin (her frantic guitar, her edgy elocution)—subtly repositioned from the perspective of an aspiring artist moving to LA—suggests that her persona tells this cautionary tale because she *does* have the do-re-mi, the cachet, the cunning and courage, but she's ambivalent; she knows how to use it, but she'd prefer not to.

Now, Ani *did* have the do-re-mi to come out as a queer figure from the outset; her self-titled debut LP of 1990 opens with "Both Hands," which endures as an anthem of queer love. Unlike the vast majority of queer musicians and celebrities whose fame preceded their public acknowledgment of their queerness, Ani immediately confronted the music industry's misogyny and homophobia—composing songs that uncompromisingly portray her position as bisexual, gender-bending, sex-positive, radical feminist—consistently questioning and queering hetero-patriarchal bureaucracies.

Oddly enough, my introduction to Ani's voice arrived by way of a rather mainstream medium: the romantic comedy of 1997, *My Best Friend's Wedding* (starring Julia Roberts), featuring Ani's cover of Hal David and Burt Bacharach's "Wishin' and Hopin'" in the opening credits. Originally recorded by Dionne Warwick as the B-side on her single "The Empty Place" of 1962, "Wishin' and Hopin'" encourages blithe deference to hetero-patriarchy: the antithesis of Ani's ethics.

4. TORI

Above all the seventy-plus Tori Amos B-sides that saved my life in adolescence, her rarity "Merman" especially helped me survive high school.

Tori told *Attitude* magazine in 1999: "When I was touring last year and Matthew Shepard got murdered I was dedicating it to him. A lot of guys were asking me to sing it for him and it just kinda took a life on of its own." I encountered this anecdote, which led me to "Merman," by browsing the now-defunct website, hereinmyhead.com—a compendium of lyrics and anecdotes for every known song written by Tori—named in tribute to "Here. In My Head," the B-side on the Australian, French, German, and UK editions of Tori's single of 1992, "Crucify" (from her debut LP, *Little Earthquakes*). I knew "Merman" was dedicated to Matthew Shepard even before I learned the lyrics—which I'd then learn before I'd hear the melody.

Initially available as a free download accompanying the online pre-order for Tori's LP of 1998, *From the Choirgirl Hotel*, the studio recording of "Merman" also appeared on the fundraiser compilation of 1999, *No Boundaries: A Benefit for the Kosovar Refugees*—and then, in 2006, on *A Piano: The Collection*, Tori's five-disc box set comprising demos, outtakes, remixes, rarities, and B-sides—while two different demo recordings of "Merman" surfaced online in 2010. But in 1999, the tune wasn't so easy for me to obtain.

The subject of "Merman" seems to suffer oppression for their queerness; the speaker alternately comforts the suffering subject and challenges the oppressor.

> *He's a merman to the knee*
> *And doesn't need something you're not willing to give*

He's a merman
Doesn't need your voice to cross his land of ice.

I daydreamed of singing these words to my bullies.

5. PJ

"Sweeter Than Anything," a B-side on the UK edition of PJ Harvey's single for "A Perfect Day Elise" (from her LP of 1998, *Is This Desire?*), required rigorous sleuthing to track down. Once again, I'd learned the lyrics, posted on a still-active fan website, alwaysontherun.net, before hearing the melody. Finding and downloading that file felt like finally meeting someone in person after a prolonged online flirtation. Today, I effortlessly search for and find "Sweeter Than Anything." As it plays, I'm fifteen again—riding the school bus, listening to this song on a mixed CD in a Discman—obsessing about an online flirtation with someone who I'd meet once and then never see again.

6. PATTI

In November 1974, Patti Smith debuted the single "Hey Joe," a perennially covered song of uncertain authorship—popularized by Jimi Hendrix in 1966, as his debut single with the Jimi Hendrix Experience—and recorded by Patti at Electric Lady Studios, the recording studio founded by Hendrix in 1970, in Manhattan.

Guitarists Lenny Kaye and Tom Verlaine, pianist Richard Sohl, and poet Patti rented a studio—using money loaned from Robert Mapplethorpe, to whom the single is dedicated—to record two of Patti's poems with instrumental accompaniment. One poem prefaces the rendition of "Hey Joe," and the second appears as the B-side, "Piss Factory."

Backed by the bop of piano and the funk of guitars, the rebellious narrator of "Piss Factory" reminisces about her first job at age sixteen—working at the fictional, eponymous factory—and her determination not to let labor exploitation oppress her visceral artistic ambitions.

At age sixteen, I'd drive to my first job in my station wagon with all the windows down, blasting the volume of the mixed CDs in my Discman, which connected to a cassette adapter in the tape player. At the bakery where I worked, I'd scrawl poems on Guest Check order pads and stash the papers in the pocket of my apron. I'd blast the volume of those mixed CDs, in the boom box behind the cash register, during closing time.

Icon and iconoclast, Patti had eluded me in early adolescence, but her ubiquity within certain spaces around New York City was immediately perceptible upon my arrival at eighteen.

Now, how often have I gazed up reverently at the Chelsea Hotel, with "Because the Night," the Patti Smith Group's single of 1978, playing on a loop in my mind?

"Piss Factory" is a recent favorite; I didn't discover it until my mid-thirties. Here, Patti's twenty-eight-year-old voice exclaims, via these words of her sixteen-year-old narrator:

> *I'm gonna go on that train to New York City,*
> *I'm gonna be somebody...*

If I'd known this B-side at eighteen, I would've played it through the open windows of my station wagon on the way out of my hometown.

ACKNOWLEDGMENTS

Eric Dean Wilson: This book is because of you. Thank you for believing in me. I believe in you. Love forever.

Eric Obenauf: This is a book because of you. Thank you again and again and again. "After the final no there comes a yes / And on that yes the future world depends" (Wallace Stevens). With your yes, my world begins. "Hop Along" is dedicated to you.

So much gratitude to Eliza Wood-Obenauf, for the love and support and the absolute joy of working together; to Brett Gregory, who felt like kin immediately upon our meeting and who completes the dream team that is Two Dollar Radio, my dream home; and to Sam Risak, copy editor extraordinaire, for the most attentive care and for guiding me to find the truest ways to say what I had to say.

Chan Marshall, you are the inspiration. Thank you, I love you.

To Hilton Als, Wayne Koestenbaum, Paul Lisicky, Lynn Melnick, Eileen Myles, and Carl Phillips, so much love and gratitude—for your faith and generosity, for all you've shared with the world, and for all I've learned from your good, hard work.

Jared Buckhiester, thank you for seeing and believing the way you do.

Jamie Fitzpatrick, thank you for hearing and believing the way you do.

Thank you, Danniel Schoonebeek, for so many years of friendship and for publishing an early draft of "Could We" in *The Fanzine*. Thank you, Jess Bergman, for editing and publishing early drafts of both "Massage the History" in *Literary Hub* and "I Sing to Use the Waiting" in *The Baffler*. Thanks to Brian Alessandro for publishing an early draft of "My Tattoos" in *The New Engagement* and to Rick Whitaker for publishing an early draft of "Is Language a Virus?" in *Exquisite Pandemic*. Thanks to Meghan O'Rourke and Spencer Lee Lenfield for editing and publishing an early draft of "Daddy Was a Musician" in *The Yale Review*. And thanks to Jackie Clark for publishing "Black Is the Colour of my True Love's Hair" in *Wendy's Subway*.

Malaga Baldi, thank you for believing and trying—and giving me the faith to try for myself. "B-Sides & Rarities" is dedicated to you.

To my friend who constantly saves my life, Angelo Nikolopoulos, and to my niece, Nico, love and gratitude.

To Ian Spencer Bell, a friend of mine, love and gratitude.

To Nicholas Cizek, thanks for the greatest encouragement. Thanks to Norma Barksdale, especially for the word "amusement."

Love and gratitude, champagne and flowers, to Chia-Lun Chang and Haoyan of America, Emily Skillings and Alex Kennedy-Grant, Wendy Xu and Jonathan Larson.

Love and gratitude to the Kearney family: Anne, Richard, Sarah, and my dear Simone.

Love and gratitude to Peter Harrington and Ichabod, to Julie Harrington and Roby Harrington and Tice.

Special thanks and so much love to Darrell Crawford and David McConnell.

So much love and gratitude to Peter Gillis.

Love and gratitude to Kim Back, Julia Berner-Tobin, Mark Bibbins, Christopher Bollen, Jamie Brisick, Michael Carroll, Rachel Cohen, CA

Conrad, Rach Crawford, Timothy Donnelly, Jack Dunnington, Andrew Durbin, Jarrett Earnest, Monica Ferrell, Jack Ferver, Matthea Harvey, Nick Holliday, Judy Hottensen, Marie Howe, Jeremy Jacob, William Johnson, Joseph Kaplan, Joan Larkin, Jessica Laser, Dorothea Lasky, Riis/Rickey Laurentiis, Paul Legault, Matthew Leifheit, Elise Lemire, Kathleen McCormick, Stephen Motika, Gaura Narayan, Ben Pease, Dan Poppick, Ali Power, Daphne Reese, Ariana Reines, Martha Rhodes, Karen Rowe, Patrick Ryan, Ira Silverberg, Diane Slocum, Ronnie Stockin, Bianca Stone, June Townsend, Nico Turner, Edmund White, Eliza Woods-Harrison, Kim Wylie, Louise Yelin, Samantha Zighelboim.

So much love and gratitude to my family: Joe, Kay, Sammy, and Lena Kleinberg and Dave Schummer; Naomi, Adi, and Nava Kidon; Miriam, Jimmy, Sarah Lena, and Jacob McLachlan; Lauren and Sam Salvay. All love and thanks to you, Rebecca Sue.

NOTES

Epigraph: Emily Dickinson, *The Complete Poems of Emily Dickinson*, ed. Thomas H. Johnson (Little, Brown, 1960).

DADDY WAS A MUSICIAN

Page 3: "*whatever* is at odds with the normal…": David M. Halperin, *Saint Foucault: Towards a Gay Hagiography* (Oxford University Press, 1995).

Page 5: "Your ideas about who you are…": *The Celluloid Closet*, directed by Rob Epstein and Jeffrey Friedman (Sony Pictures Classics, 1996).

Page 5: "The idea of homosexuality first emerged onscreen…": Vito Russo, *The Celluloid Closet: Homosexuality in the Movies, Revised Edition* (Harper & Row, 1987).

Page 6: "microvariations"…"tend to make their *S*…": *Do I Sound Gay?*, directed by David Thorpe (IFC Films, 2014).

Page 7: "a kid is identifying…": Ibid.

Page 7: "The break between registers…": Wayne Koestenbaum, *The Queen's Throat: Opera, Homosexuality, and the Mystery of Desire* (Da Capo Press, 2001; originally published 1993).

Page 9: *My daddy was a musician…*: Cat Power, "My Daddy Was a Musician," *duyster*, Studio Brussel, Brussels, Belgium, aired February 23, 2003 (recorded January 2003).

Page 9: *My father was a gamblin' man…*: The Animals, "The House of the Rising Sun," *The Animals* (MGM Records, 1964).

Page 9: *My father was a music man…*: Cat Power, "House of the Rising Sun," *Live Session EP* (iTunes Exclusive; Matador Records, 2006).

Page 10: "[The] Amateur renews his pleasure…": Roland Barthes, *Roland Barthes by Roland Barthes*, tr. Richard Howard (Farrar, Straus & Giroux, 1977).

Page 10: "Listening, we are the ideal mother…": Koestenbaum, op. cit.

Page 11: "The gestures of a singer…": Ibid.

Page 11: "[My] body produces homosexuality…": Ibid.

Page 13: "a positionality that is not restricted…": Halperin, op. cit.

Page 13: "envision a variety of possibilities…": Ibid.

Page 13: *It is the law of my own voice I shall investigate…*: Frank O'Hara, "Homosexuality," *The Collected Poems of Frank O'Hara*, ed. Donald Allen (University of California Press, 1971).

MY TATTOOS

Page 18: "tradition"… "in the particular sense of 'reception'…": Harold Bloom, *Kabbalah and Criticism* (Continuum, 2005; originally published 1975)

Page 18: "a devout Jew with leanings toward mysticism…": Gershom Scholem, *Kabbalah* (Plume, 1978; originally published 1974).

Page 18: "the divine emanations by which all reality is structured…": Bloom, op. cit.

Page 19: "The *Zohar* is organized as an apparent commentary…": Ibid.

Page 19: "an immutable knowledge of a final reality…": Ibid.

Page 19: "return through mystic communion…": Scholem, op. cit.

Page 20: "rhetorical series of techniques for opening Scripture…": Bloom, op. cit.

Page 20: "In its degeneracy, Kabbalah has sought…": Ibid.

Page 23: "Kabbalah says the Bible is a complete code…": Yehuda Berg, *The 72 Names of God: Technology for the Soul* (Kabbalah Publishing, 2004).

Page 23: "What attracted you to it?"…"I was looking for something…": Larry King, *Larry King Live*, aired October 10, 2002, CNN.

Page 24: "Kabbalah unravels all the mysteries…": Yehuda Berg, *The Red String Book: The Power of Protection* (Kabbalah Publishing, 2004).

Page 25: *Words are useless…*: Madonna, "Bedtime Story," *Bedtime Stories* (Maverick/Sire Records/Warner Bros. Records, 1994).

Page 26: *I saw the lights, and I was on my way…*: Madonna, "Lament," *Evita: The Complete Motion Picture Soundtrack* (Warner Bros. Records, 1996).

Page 27: *Touch me, I'm dying*: Madonna, "Skin," *Ray of Light* (Maverick/Warner Bros. Records, 1998).

Page 27: "Her voice wasn't strong…": Kim Gordon, *Girl in a Band* (Dey Street Books, 2015).

MASSAGE THE HISTORY

Page 31: "Whatever is fitted in any sort to excite the ideas of pain…": Edmund Burke, *A Philosophical Enquiry into the Origin of Our Ideas of the Sublime and the Beautiful* (Oxford University Press, 2015; originally published 1757).

Page 31: "the sensation which accompanies the removal of pain or danger…": Burke, op. cit.

Page 32: "California is a place of death…": Kim Gordon, *Girl in a Band* (Dey Street Books, 2015).

Page 33: "*the sensation of the 'eternal'…*": Romain Rolland, letter to Sigmund Freud, December 5, 1927; quoted in David James Fisher, *Romain Rolland and the Politics of Intellectual Engagement* (University of California Press, 1988).

Page 33: "the intimate union of the ego with the surrounding world…": Julia Kristeva, *This Incredible Need to Believe*, tr. Beverley Bie Brahic (Columbia University Press, 2011; originally published 2009).

Page 33: "losing the boundaries of the self…": Kristeva, op. cit.

Page 33: "Positive and negative, joy and extreme pain…": Ibid.

Page 34: "blueprints for a future Sonic Youth album…": Stuart Berman, "Sonic Youth: Simon Werner a Disparu OST Album

Review," Pitchfork, February 21, 2011, pitchfork.com/reviews/albums/15119-simon-werner-a-disparu-ost.

Page 35: *I'm not afraid to say I'm scared...*: Sonic Youth, "The Burning Spear," *Sonic Youth* (Neutral Records, 1982).

Page 35: "Fear being an apprehension of pain or death...": Burke, op. cit.

Page 35: *Look before you leap, OK...*: Sonic Youth, "I Dreamed I Dream," *Sonic Youth* (Neutral Records, 1982).

Page 35: *Are you gonna liberate us girls from male, white, corporate oppression...*: Sonic Youth, "Kool Thing," *Goo* (DGC Records, 1990).

Page 36: "She has a distinctly physical response to language...": Hilton Als, in Kim Gordon, *Performing/Guzzling* (Rizzoli, 2010).

Page 36: "Another source of the sublime, is *infinity*"... "Infinity has a tendency to fill the mind with that sort of delightful horror...": Burke, op. cit.

Page 37: "madmen"... "remain whole days and nights...": Ibid.

Page 37: *All the money's gone...*: Sonic Youth, "I Dreamed I Dream," op. cit; Sonic Youth, "Massage the History," *The Eternal* (Matador Records, 2009).

Page 37: *But it was never here...*: Sonic Youth, "Massage the History," op. cit.

Page 37: *Oil dripping on my head...*: Ibid.

Page 38: "Something's really at stake in this performance...": Ben Ratliff, "Critics' Choice – New CDs – Review," *The New York Times*, June 8, 2009.

Page 38: *I want you to suck my neck...*: Sonic Youth, "Massage the History," op. cit.

Page 39: "the creator of the primal scream...": Gordon, op. cit.

Page 39: *Look to the right, lemme get a close-up...*: Peaches (feat. Kim Gordon), "Close Up," *Rub* (I U She Music, 2015).

Page 40: *black matte spray...*: Kim Gordon, "Murdered Out," *Murdered Out – Single* (Matador Records, 2016).

Page 40: "It's almost like a peaceful resistance...": Maria Sherman, "Hear Kim Gordon's First Song Released Under Her Own Name," NPR, September 12, 2016,

npr.org/sections/therecord/2016/09/12/493259751/
hear-kim-gordons-first-song-released-under-her-own-name.

Page 40: "Even though Sonic Youth is associated with it"… "When I saw and heard No Wave bands…": Gordon, op. cit.

Page 41: "Astonishment is that state of the soul"… "The effect of the sublime in the highest degree…": Burke, op. cit.

Page 41: *Getting dizzy, sitting around, Sacred Trickster and a no-tech sound…*: Sonic Youth, "Sacred Trickster," *The Eternal* (Matador Records, 2009).

Page 41: *What's it like to be a girl in a band…*: Ibid.

COULD WE

Page 44: "We would get into the studio and I would play a song…": Alex Wagner, "The Last Call," The Fader, January 26, 2006, thefader.com/2006/01/26/greatest-hits.

Page 46: *Could we? Take a walk?…*: Cat Power, "Could We," *The Greatest* (Matador Records, 2006).

Page 46: "Dinette, will you *please* hush?"…"I gotta slow down"…: Chan Marshall, May 4, 2004, The Earl, Atlanta, GA.

Page 47: *I hate myself… and I want to die…*: Cat Power, "Hate," *The Greatest* (Matador Records, 2006).

Page 47: "a column of air": *No Direction Home: Bob Dylan*, directed by Martin Scorsese (Spitfire Pictures/Grey Water Park Productions/Thirteen/WNET New York/Sikelia Productions, 2005).

Page 48: *I do not hate myself and I do not want to die…*: Chan Marshall, August 25, 2006, Malibu Performing Arts Center, Los Angeles, CA; Cat Power, "Unhate," *Covers* (Domino Recording Company, 2022).

Page 48: "I just love reverb on the vocal"…"That sucked": Marshall, August 25, 2006, op. cit.

Page 49: "Did I play this one yet"…"It's hard to sing when it's real tight like that…": Chan Marshall, September 5, 2006, Boston Museum of Fine Arts, Boston, MA.

Page 50: "the most amazing reverb"…"That was probably the first time I performed…": Chan Marshall, *aspekte*, filmed June 22, 2013, ZDF.

Page 50: "Now that we've been playing live…": Chan Marshall, *Austin City Limits*, filmed September 18, 2006, Austin PBS/KLRU-TV.

Page 50: *He's related to you…*: Cat Power, "Nude as the News," *What Would the Community Think* (Matador Records, 1996).

Page 51: *Unbelievable things… Hater, I have your diamonds…*: Cat Power, "Cross Bones Style," *Moon Pix* (Matador Records, 1998).

Page 52: *Let's make another date real soon, in the afternoon…*: Cat Power, "Could We," op. cit.

Page 52: "That's a song about doin' it in the afternoon…": Chan Marshall, October 22, 2006, The Earl, Atlanta, GA.

Page 52: *the later parade…*: Cat Power, "The Greatest," *The Greatest* (Matador Records, 2006).

Page 52: "I guess the guitar never came…": Chan Marshall, Vegoose, October 28, 2006, Snake Eyes Stage, Las Vegas, NV.

Page 53: "Sad and groovy…": Chan Marshall, Rencontres Trans Musicales, December 7, 2006, Parc Expo Rennes Aeroport, Rennes.

Page 54: *Who's gonna play drums, guitar, or organ with chorus…*: Cat Power, "Lived in Bars," *The Greatest* (Matador Records, 2006).

Page 54: "I wish it was louder…": Chan Marshall, Rencontres Trans Musicales, op. cit.

Page 55: *Would you let me walk down your street…*: Moby Grape, "Naked, If I Want To," *Moby Grape* (Columbia Records, 1967).

Page 55: *Could we…*: Cat Power, "Could We," op. cit.

Page 55: *When I'm driving in my car…*: The Rolling Stones, "(I Can't Get No) Satisfaction," *(I Can't Get No) Satisfaction* (London Records, 1965).

Page 55: *When you see me walking down the street…*: Smokey Robinson and the Miracles, "The Tracks of My Tears," *Going to a Go-Go* (Tamla, 1965).

Page 55: "Ladies and gentlemen, brothers and sisters…": Gregg Foreman, Primavera Sound, May 30, 2008, Barcelona.

Page 56: "Five albums that made me who I am at forty…": Cat Power, "Five Albums That Shaped Chan's Life," Spotify

Audio Interview, September 10, 2012, open.spotify.com/album/3ixI02xdtyyrjGdB1Yc3Vk.

Page 56: "The first song on that record is called 'These Arms of Mine'...": Ibid.

Page 56: "That's the one that electrocuted my brain...": Ibid.

Page 56: "the mechanical properties of your head...": Timothy E. Hullar, "Why does my voice sound so different when it is recorded and played back?," *Scientific American*, January 13, 2009.

Page 57: "I sing to use the Waiting...": Emily Dickinson, *The Complete Poems of Emily Dickinson*, ed. Thomas H. Johnson (Little, Brown, 1960).

I SING TO USE THE WAITING

Page 60: "You need a theme song...": *Ally McBeal*, season 1, episode 17, "Theme of Life," directed by Dennie Gordon, written by David E. Kelley, aired March 9, 1998, Fox Broadcasting Company.

Page 61: "obsessive-compulsive disorder / with acute musical-obsessive disorder...": Jeremy O. Harris, *Slave Play* (Theatre Communications Group, 2020).

Page 62: "It didn't sound the way it normally does...": Ibid.

Page 62: "persistent sounds or tunes...": Juan Manuel Orjuela Rojas and Ingrid Lizeth Lizarazo Rodríguez, "The Stuck Song Syndrome: A Case of Musical Obsessions," *American Journal of Case Reports* 19 (November 2018): 1329–33.

Page 62–3: "Our best explanation is that the neural circuits representing a song get stuck in 'playback mode'...": Daniel J. Levitan, *This Is Your Brain on Music: The Science of a Human Obsession* (Dutton, 2006).

Page 63: "Is it some oddity of sound, of timbre or rhythm or melody...": Oliver Sacks, *Musicophilia: Tales of Music and the Brain* (Vintage, 2007).

Page 63: "The recurring tune may announce in its compelling and compulsive pressure the working of an unknown power in you...": Theodor Reik, *The Haunting Melody: Psychoanalytic Experiences in Life and Music* (Grove Press, 1960).

Page 64: "journey to the Day…": Emily Dickinson, *The Complete Poems of Emily Dickinson*, ed. Thomas H. Johnson (Little, Brown, 1960).

TOO GOOD TO WORK

Page 65: "I wanted to have a year to just do whatever I want…": Abby Aguire, "It's Rihanna's World," *Vogue*, March 17, 2016.

Page 66: "When you're an older lady"… "Remembered as Rihanna…": "Rihanna Predicts Her Own Future," MTV News, mtv.com/video-clips/sxm155/rihanna-predicts-her-own-future.

Page 67: "It is during the early and ensuing decades on the plantation…": Curwen Best, *The Popular Music and Entertainment Culture of Barbados: Pathways to Digital Culture* (Scarecrow Press, 2012).

Page 68: "jive, jitterbugging, 'jogging,' arm-swinging, rolling, hip-wagging, shaking and waltzing…": Sonjah Stanley Niaah, *DanceHall: From Slave Ship to Ghetto* (University of Ottawa Press, 2010).

Page 68: "The recoding of the mainstream perception of the margin…": Ibid.

Page 69: "A pop-dancehall number that's all bubble and no depth…": Jon Caramanica, "Review: Rihanna, Blissfully Adrift, Juggles Styles on 'Anti,'" *The New York Times*, January 28, 2016, nytimes.com/2016/01/29/arts/music/review-rihanna-blissfully-adrift-juggles-styles-on-anti.html.

Page 69: *Yeah, OK…*: Rihanna (feat. Drake), "Work," *Anti* (Westbury Road Entertainment/Roc Nation, 2016).

Page 70: "The track draws upon the warm island pop of her earlier material…": "Rihanna feat. Drake, 'What's My Name,'" Billboard, November 19, 2010, billboard.com/music/music-news/rihanna-feat-drake-whats-my-name-1068420.

Page 71: *Oh na-na… looking for a guy to put in work…*: Rihanna (feat. Drake), "What's My Name?," *Loud* (Def Jam Recordings/SRP Records, 2010).

Page 71: *I'll get high if I want to…*: Drake (feat. Rihanna), "Take Care," *Take Care* (Young Money Entertainment/Cash Money Records/Universal Republic Records, 2011).

Page 71: *good weed, white wine...*: Rihanna, "What's My Name?," op. cit.

Page 72: "While mainstream critics may be uncomfortable...": Taj Rani, "How Rihanna's 'Work' Made Dancehall Reign in Pop (Again)," Billboard, March 2, 2016, billboard.com/music/pop/rihanna-work-dancehall-essay-6889497.

Page 73: "The addition of Caribbean queen Rihanna...": Katie Atkinson, "Billboard's 100 Best Pop Songs of 2016: Critics' Picks," Billboard, December 12, 2016, billboard.com/music/music-news/billboard-top-100-pop-songs-of-2016-7617635.

Page 73: *I got high as the expectations... work too hard... I'm too good for you...*: Drake (feat. Rihanna), "Too Good," *Views* (Young Money Entertainment/Cash Money Records/Universal Republic Records, 2016).

BALLAD OF ROBYN AND WHITNEY

Page 76: "She introduced herself as 'Whitney Elizabeth Houston'...": Robyn Crawford, "Whitney Elizabeth Houston, 1963–2012," *Esquire*, February 12, 2012, esquire.com/entertainment/music/a12753/whitney-houston-6654718.

Page 76: "my and Whitney's dream...": Robyn Crawford, *A Song for You: My Life with Whitney Houston* (Dutton, 2019).

Page 77: "She looked like an angel...": Crawford, "Whitney Elizabeth Houston," op. cit.

Page 77: "My mother always says...": *Whitney*, directed by Kevin Macdonald (Lisa Erspamer Entertainment/Lightbox, 2018).

Page 77: "She worked her ass off...": Ibid.

Page 78: "I taught Whitney...": *Whitney: Can I Be Me*, directed by Nick Broomfield and Rudi Dolezal (Lafayette Films/Passion Pictures/Showtime Networks, 2017).

Page 78: "When you're raised in church...": Ibid.

Page 78: "For a small child [the] parents are at first the only authority...": Sigmund Freud, "Family Romances," in *The Freud Reader*, ed. Peter Gay (W. W. Norton & Company, 1989).

Page 79: "I had wanted to know the Word for myself...": Crawford, *A Song for You*, op. cit.

Page 79: "Her life was organized around going to church...": Ibid.

Page 79: "I was too worried to stay...": Ibid.

Page 80: "On that day, I sat in that church...": Ibid.

Page 80: "talk music and scripture for hours"... "I continued to read the Bible on my own...": Ibid.

Page 80: "The psychological changes that regularly succeed the prolonged distress of separation...": John Bowlby, *Attachment and Loss, Volume One: Attachment, Second Edition* (Basic Books, 1983).

Page 81: "everybody in the family except Cissy"... "an opportunist...": *Whitney*, op. cit.

Page 82: "Rumors had already started about her sexuality...": *Whitney: Can I Be Me*, op. cit.

Page 82: "She was something that I didn't want my sister to be involved with...": *Whitney*, op. cit.

Page 83: "We have each, at some time in our lives...": Sarah Schulman, *Ties That Bind: Familial Homophobia and Its Consequences* (The New Press, 2009).

Page 83: "They are being controlled by a broad, yet invisible, social force...": Ibid.

Page 83: "a reversed value in which it is the homophobe who is destroying the family...": Ibid.

Page 84: "Whitney came by my mother's apartment...": Crawford, *A Song for You*, op. cit.

Page 84: "Whitney said, 'I wish I could be two places at once'...": Ibid.

Page 84: "Her mother didn't like it at all...": Ibid.

Page 84: "That story altered the professional landscape...": Ibid.

Page 86–7: "very stoned"..."I hate her": *The Bodyguard*, directed by Mick Jackson (Warner Bros., 1992).

Page 87: "She slept with me in that bed...": *Whitney*, op. cit.

Page 88: "In the beginning, she was a good parent...": Ibid.

Page 88: "All Kristina ever wanted...": Crawford, *A Song for You*, op. cit.

Page 88: "destroy herself": *Whitney: Can I Be Me*, op. cit.

Page 89: "Whitney's character was Savannah...": Ibid.

Page 89: "My father's a queer...": *Waiting to Exhale*, directed by Forest Whitaker (20th Century Fox, 1995).

Page 89: "Every woman needs a man...": Ibid.

Page 90: "I'm smart, I work hard...": Ibid.

Page 90: "It's all right...": Ibid.

Page 90: "I don't want her murdered...": Crawford, *A Song for You*, op. cit.

Page 90: "the threat of bodily harm...": Ibid.

Page 91: "That's my mom...": *The Preacher's Wife*, directed by Penny Marshall (Touchstone Pictures/The Samuel Goldwyn Company, 1996).

Page 91: "That's my grandma...": Ibid.

Page 92: "Bobbi Kris and I have a great relationship...": *Whitney: Can I Be Me*, op. cit.

Page 93: "I'm assuming [the family] paid her off...": Ibid.

Page 93: "'You don't buy a gift for a man from my wife'"..."I understood exactly why I was getting blasted...": Crawford, *A Song for You*, op. cit.

Page 94: "I think the biggest change in her...": *Whitney: Can I Be Me*, op. cit.

Page 94: "Whitney can call Nippy...": *Whitney*, op. cit.

Page 95: *I love you in a place...*: *Welcome Home Heroes with Whitney Houston*, directed by David Mallet (Arista Records, 1991).

Page 96: "I don't know why, but Nip decided to include 'A Song for You'...": Crawford, *A Song for You*, op. cit.

Page 96: *God grant me the courage... Robyn, What an assistant!...*: Whitney Houston, *Whitney Houston* (Arista Records, 1985).

NEGLIGENT MOMS

Page 104: "Cher, who has just turned 19...": "Cher's Rise to Fame!," *KFWB Hitline* vol. 1, no. 11, issue 11, August 23, 1965; quoted in Mark Bego, *Cher: If You Believe* (Taylor Trade Publishing, 2001).

Page 104: "My father lived long enough...": Elaine Markoutsas, "Mother Wants Life to Be Better for Cher," *Chicago Tribune*, February 15, 1976; quoted in Bego, *Cher*, op. cit.

Page 105: "Moving in apparent freedom...": Pauline Kael, "The Current Cinema," *The New Yorker*, November 7, 1982.

Page 107: "I hate you going out all the time...": *Mask*, directed by Peter Bogdanovich (Universal Pictures, 1985).

Page 107: "the mirror-image would seem the threshold...": Jacques Lacan, *Écrits: The First Complete Edition in English*, tr. Bruce Fink (W. W. Norton, 2006).

Page 107: "This moment in which the mirror-stage comes to an end...": Ibid.

Page 108: "Rusty Dennis is played by Cher...": Roger Ebert, "Mask," rogerebert.com/reviews/mask-1985 (originally published March 22, 1985).

Page 108: "I don't know why people are preoccupied...": Kevin Sessums, "Cher Starred and Feathered," *Vanity Fair*, November 1990, archive.vanityfair.com/article/1990/11/cher-starred-and-feathered.

Page 110: "I miss my father...": *Mermaids*, directed by Richard Benjamin (Orion Pictures, 1990).

Page 111: "You kissed her...": Ibid.

Page 111: "Thumb-sucking is determined...": Sigmund Freud, *Three Essays on the Theory of Sexuality*, in *The Freud Reader*, ed. Peter Gay (W. W. Norton & Company, 1989).

Page 111: "makes [the child] independent of the external world...": Ibid.

Page 112: "kissing your hand...": *Mermaids*, op. cit.

Page 112: "What's your major, town tramp...": Ibid.

Page 113: "You know, you're just one year younger than I was...": Ibid.

Page 113: "sum total of everything the actors have been affected by...": Kael, "The Current Cinema," op. cit.

Page 113: "Cher's new film, *Mermaids*…": Sessums, "Cher Starred and Feathered," op. cit.

Page 114: "I was hysterical one day…": *Becoming Chaz*, directed by Fenton Bailey and Randy Barbato (World of Wonder Productions, 2011).

Page 114: "I don't know why people are preoccupied…": Sessums, "Cher Starred and Feathered," op. cit.

Page 115: "What do you think about the fact that we sound so much alike…": *Dear Mom, Love Cher*, directed by P. David Ebersole (Lifetime, 2013).

Page 115: "Look for Cher & mom sing 'I'm just your yesterday.'…": Cher (@cher), Twitter/X, December 13, 2022.

IS LANGUAGE A VIRUS?

Page 121: "My general theory since 1971…": William S. Burroughs, "Ten Years and a Billion Dollars," in *The Adding Machine: Collected Essays* (Grove Press, 1985).

Page 121: "Pain cry…": Anderson, "Language Is a Virus," op. cit.

Page 121: "word dust drifted from outer space…": William S. Burroughs, *Nova Express* (Grove Press, 1964).

Page 122: "This is a quote from William Burroughs…": Laurie Anderson, interview with the Warner Bros. Music Show, 1986.

Page 122: "You know his redundancies are numerous…": Ira Silverberg, personal correspondence, January 14, 2021.

Page 123: "Language is a skin…": Roland Barthes, *A Lovers Discourse: Fragments*, tr. Richard Howard (Farrar, Straus and Giroux, 1978).

Page 123: "rub out the word forever…": Burroughs, *Nova Express*, op cit.

HOP ALONG; OR, THE PRONOUN "THEY"

Page 126: *Hop along, sing your song*…: Hop Along, Queen Ansleis, "For Sebastian, from a Friend," *Freshman Year* (self-released, 2006)

Page 127: "When female singers use this lowest register…": Acoustical Society of America, "Why Vocal Fry?," May 24, 2016, sciencedaily.com/releases/2016/05/160524121533.htm.

Page 128: "the rasp"… "If *Pablo Honey* Radiohead…": Jesse David Fox, "Is This the Best Voice in Rock Music Today?," Vulture, May 8, 2015, vulture.com/2015/05/this-the-best-voice-in-rock-music-today.html.

Page 129: *Queen Ansleis is about to jump…*: Hop Along, "Junkyard James," *Is Something Wrong?* (self-released, 2009).

Page 132: *That boy is an armed man, bearing flowers and two hands…*: Hop Along, Queen Ansleis, "Bruno Is Orange," *Freshman Year* (self-released, 2006).

Page 133: *I had to shoot that dog you loved so much…*: Hop Along, "Sister Cities," *Painted Shut* (Saddle Creek, 2015).

Page 134: "I've come to understand (better) why I felt so compelled to start going by my middle name when I turned 18…": Frances Quinlan (@francq__), Twitter/X, January 22, 2021.

COLORS OF THE WIND

Page 141: *You think I'm an ignorant savage…*: Judy Kuhn, "Colors of the Wind," *Pocahontas: An Original Walt Disney Records Soundtrack* (Walt Disney Records, 1995).

Page 141: "In the song, I basically wanted…": "Stephen Schwartz Comments on Disney's Pocahontas," 2010, stephenschwartz.com/wp-content/uploads/2017/05/Disney-Pocahontas.pdf.

Page 141: "There's an earthiness to her voice…": Playbill, "Judy Kuhn Takes You Inside the Music of Disney's Pocahontas," April 22, 2019, youtube.com/watch?v=hzwW6bQDUx4.

Page 142: "The verse that takes you to the song proper…": Ibid.

Page 142: "very likely spurious…": Jerry L. Clark, "Thus Spoke Chief Seattle: The Story of An Undocumented Speech," *Prologue Magazine* 18, no. 1 (Spring 1985).

Page 143: "If you kill him…": *Pocahontas*, directed by Mike Gabriel and Eric Goldberg (Walt Disney Pictures/Walt Disney Animation Studios, 1995).

Page 144: "mother right"… "Among the Powhatans…": Paula Gunn Allen, *Pocahontas: Medicine Woman, Spy, Entrepreneur, Diplomat* (HarperCollins, 2003).

Page 144: "the answer is unequivocally no"… "Was she really the one…": Camilla Townsend, *Pocahontas and the Powhattan Dilemma* (Farrar, Straus and Giroux, 2004).

Page 145: "She is visible only in the comments"… "'In how many daies'…": Ibid.

AFTERWORD: B-SIDES & RARITIES

Page 154: "When I was touring last year…": Matthew Todd, "Tori's Glory," *Attitude*, November 1999.

Page 154–5: *He's a merman to the knee…*: Tori Amos, "Merman," *A Piano: The Collection* (Rhino Records, 2006).

Page 156: *I'm gonna go on that train to New York City…*: Patti Smith, "Piss Factory," *Hey Joe/Piss Factory* (Sire Records, 1977; originally released 1974).

Two Dollar Radio
Books too loud to Ignore

ALSO AVAILABLE Here are some other titles you might want to dig into.

THEY CAN'T KILL US UNTIL THEY KILL US ESSAYS BY **HANIF ABDURRAQIB**

→ **Best Books 2017:** NPR, *Buzzfeed*, *Paste Magazine*, *Esquire*, *Chicago Tribune*, *Vol. 1 Brooklyn*, CBC (Canada), *Stereogum*, *National Post* (Canada), *Entropy*, *Heavy*, *Book Riot*, *Chicago Review of Books* (November), *The Los Angeles Review*, *Michigan Daily*

← "Funny, painful, precise, desperate, and loving throughout. Not a day has sounded the same since I read him."
—Greil Marcus, *Village Voice*

NIGHT ROOMS ESSAYS BY **GINA NUTT**

→ **"A Best Book of 2021"** —NPR

← "In writing both revelatory and intimate, Nutt probes the most frightening aspects of life in such a way that she manages to shed light and offer understanding even about those things that lurk in the deepest and darkest of shadows." —Kristin Iversen, *Refinery29*

← "A hallucinatory experience that doesn't obscure but instead deepens the subjects that Nutt explores." —Jeannie Vanasco, *The Believer*

A HISTORY OF MY BRIEF BODY
ESSAYS BY **BILLY-RAY BELCOURT**

→ 2021 Lambda Literary Award for Gay Memoir/Biography, Finalist.
→ **"A Best Book of 2020"** —*Kirkus Reviews, Book Riot, CBC, Globe and Mail*

← "Stunning." —Michelle Hart, *O, The Oprah Magazine*

A BRAVE, RAW, AND fiercely intelligent collection of essays and vignettes on grief, colonial violence, joy, love, and queerness.

SOME OF US ARE VERY HUNGRY NOW
BY **ANDRE PERRY**

← "A complete, deep, satisfying read." —Gabino Iglesias, NPR

ANDRE PERRY'S DEBUT COLLECTION of personal essays travels from Washington DC to Iowa City to Hong Kong in search of both individual and national identity while displaying tenderness and a disarming honesty.

808S & OTHERWORLDS ESSAYS BY **SEAN AVERY MEDLIN**

→ **"September's Most Anticipated LGBTQIA+ Literature"** —*Lambda Literary*

← An elegant mash of memoir, poetry, tales of appropriation, thoughts on Black masculinity, Hulk, Kanye." —Christopher Borrelli, *Chicago Tribune*

← "Purrs with variety and energy, with riffs on Black masculinity, anime, gaming, rap, gender identity, and dislocation in Phoenix's western suburbs."
—Michelle Beaver, *The Los Angeles Review of Books*

← "Gives a voice to queer Black rap enthusiasts." —*Teen Vogue*